Routledge Revivals

Inclusive Education in Europe

Originally published in 1995, this book offers a crucial view of the implementation of legislation for the integration of pupils with special educational needs in EU countries at the time. The match or mismatch between the rhetoric and reality, between the policy and the practice are reviewed by presenters from a recent appraisal of progress in individual national contexts. Authors are critical of the situation in their own countries and call upon recent and relevant research sources to support their views. The relationships between particular themes in the education of pupils with special needs are observed and compared in a broad European context.

Inclusive Education in Europe

Edited by
Christine O'Hanlon

Routledge
Taylor & Francis Group

First published in 1995
by David Fulton Publishers

This edition first published in 2018 by Routledge
2 Park Square, Milton Park, Abingdon, Oxon OX14 4RN

and by Routledge
711 Third Avenue, New York, NY 10017

Routledge is an imprint of the Taylor & Francis Group, an informa business

Publisher's Note
The publisher has gone to great lengths to ensure the quality of this reprint but points out that some imperfections in the original copies may be apparent.

Disclaimer
The publisher has made every effort to trace copyright holders and welcomes correspondence from those they have been unable to contact.

A Library of Congress record exists under ISBN: 1853464058

ISBN: 978-1-138-30406-2 (hbk)
ISBN: 978-0-203-73040-9 (ebk)
ISBN: 978-1-138-30410-9 (pbk)

INCLUSIVE EDUCATION IN EUROPE

Dedication

Eoin, Cormac, Catherine and John

to my friends and colleagues on the ATEE sub-group and the RIF sub-network working in integration and inclusion in education who keep the debate and action in Europe moving forward.

INCLUSIVE EDUCATION IN EUROPE

Edited by
Christine O'Hanlon

David Fulton Publishers
London

David Fulton Publishers Ltd
2 Barbon Close, London WC1N 3JX

First published in Great Britain by David Fulton Publishers 1995

British Library Cataloguing in Publication Data

A catalogue record for this book is available from the British Library

ISBN 1-85346-405–8

Typeset by The Harrington Consultancy

Contents

The Contributors vi
Preface vii
Introduction *Patrick Daunt* 1
1. Denmark *Susan Tetler* 9
2. France *Felicity Armstrong* 24
3. Germany *Dirk Randoll* 39
4. Greece *V. Lampropoulou and S. Padeliaudou* 49
5. Ireland *Patricia Lynch* 61
6. Italy *Irene Menegoi Buzzi* 75
7. The Netherlands *Kees Den Boer* 82
8. Portugal *Ana Maria Bernard da Costa* 94
9. Spain *Carmen G. Pastor* 110
10. UK *Christine O'Hanlon* 122
11. Belgium *A. Dens and E. Hoedemakers* 133

The Contributors

Felicity Armstrong is a lecturer in the Division of Education, University of Sheffield, UK.

Kees Den Boer is a lecturer at the Seminarium Voor Orthopedagogiek, Utrecht, The Netherlands.

Irene Menegoi Buzzi is a lecturer at IRRSAE (Istituto Regionale di Ricerca Sperimentazione Aggiornamento Educativi), Milan, Italy.

Ana Maria Benard Da Costa works at Instituto de Inovacâo Educacional, Ministry of Education, Lisbon, Portugal.

Patrick Daunt is an International Consultant in Education and Disability, Cambridge, UK.

August Dens is Director of the Support Centre for Special Needs Education; he works with his colleague, *E. Hoedemaekers*, at the Psycho-Medisch-Sociaal Centrum, Leuven, Belgium.

Venetta Lampropoulou is a lecturer in special needs education in the Department of Education, School of Humanities and Social Sciences, University of Patras, Greece.

Patricia Lynch is a lecturer in the Department of Special Education, St Patricks College, Drumcondra, Dublin.

Christine O'Hanlon is a Senior Lecturer in Special Education and Educational Psychology in the School of Education, University of Birmingham, UK.

Carmen Garcia Pastor is a Professor in Special Education in the Facultad de Filosofia y Ciencias de la Educacion at the University of Seville, Spain.

Dirk Randoll is a research associate in the Department of Psychology at the German Institute for International Educational Research, Frankfurt am Main, Germany.

Susan Tetler is a PhD student and teacher of special education in teacher education at the Royal Danish School for Educational Studies, in Copenhagen, Denmark.

Preface

Working in the European dimension in education brings with it highs and lows. The highs are related to the achievement of collaboration in a joint venture like this book and the lows are associated with the problems linked to communication and understanding in second language contexts about complex issues like the ones addressed in this book.

It is a pleasure to be able to offer this second book on integration or inclusion of children in mainstream education in a Europe-wide context. This book questions the practical development of legislation and policy in EU countries. The book is an edited compendium of chapters offered from colleagues in 11 EU countries, with the exception of Chapter 1 which is an introduction by Patrick Daunt who is closely connected to the advancement of policy and practice for people with disabilities in Europe.

Each contributor offers a unique and 'insider' view of what 'integration' or 'inclusion' means to them in a national context. Felicity Armstrong is writing about France from her extensive experience and knowledge of the situation and takes more of an 'outsider' perspective. The chapter from Belgium is written as a case study of an integration experiment. All contributors deliberately bring a critical perspective to their writing, because so often the standard sanitized version of what is hoped for or is intended to happen in each country is offered as an apology for lack of action. This book seeks to uncover the real country response to the policy directives on inclusive education in recent years.

As editor I had the problem of coordinating the different terminology for the sake of the reader's understanding. A number of contributors originally used the terms 'the handicapped' and 'handicapped children' which I have changed to 'people with disabilities', 'children with handicaps' or 'pupils with special educational needs' (SEN) where appropriate. Other terms such as 'severe learning difficulties', may be used in a sense which is more akin to children with learning difficulties in the UK. I also substitute the term 'mainstream' where appropriate and in liaison with the original terminology of 'normal', 'ordinary', 'regular', and 'state' school used in the original.

A certain amount of rewriting was necessary in many chapters, because a number of contributors were writing in a second language, therefore the expression of their ideas was in need of further development after the translation. As a result, the book is offered with some transformation of the original texts but with, I hope the original and authentic meaning of the author retained.

Each chapter reflects the personal views of the writers within their national contexts. I take this opportunity to thank all contributors for their excellent work and the time necessary on everyone's part to reach this satisfactory conclusion.

Christine O'Hanlon

Introduction: Integration Practice and Policy for Children with Special Needs in Europe

Patrick Daunt

It is among the many merits of this book that it gives us a chapter for each of the countries, apart from Luxembourg, in membership of the European Union before the recent accession. With the exception of the Belgian contribution, which consists of a specific case study, the chapters comprise country reports, interesting comparisons being made possible by accounts which cover much the same range of issues and ground of policy. As a bonus, we find particularly informative and thoughtful treatments of Greece, Ireland and Portugal, countries whose situations are less frequently or fully reported.

Readers may find themselves struck less by the fruitful valleys of commonality than by the harsh peaks of divergence. In Denmark 'only half per cent of the students in the primary and secondary school have been educated outside an ordinary school environment' (Tetler). In The Netherlands, '95 per cent of the children with special educational needs...attend a special school' (Den Boer) – and that is at primary level; in France (Armstrong), apart from children with 'social handicaps', 48 per cent of children with disabilities live and learn (or rather, do not learn) beyond the pale of the Education Ministry. For Tetler 'the idea of a common norm applied to all students in school now seems to be abandoned'; the news of this does not appear to have reached the Department for Education in London.

On the other hand, most contributors acknowledge the arrival of a new conceptual weapon of common interest, the idea of the 'inclusive school', accredited with international authority since UNESCO's 1994 Salamanca world conference. Many of the components of this notion – flexibility, openness, individualization, team-teaching, project work, and so on will be familiar to those who were engaged in curriculum development in the 1960s. We are endeavouring, evidently, to recapture ground then won but since for many of us substantially lost, with the hope of advancing further into quite new territory. In important ways, our forces are much stronger than they were then: there are at least some signs of greater parental commitment to the cause, specialized teachers and other professionals are potentially powerful new allies, and the children with special needs themselves, previously not even recruited, now form the vanguard. But the defenders of discriminatory education, caught generally by surprise 30 years ago, now hold entrenched positions.

It must not be supposed that this implies among the authors here a triumphalist crusading spirit. Where there is optimism it is expressed with caution and moderation. In so far as attitudes are crucial, studies indicate that among parents, teachers and heads, 'the most important factor is already in place in Irish schools' (Lynch). The 1994 Act of the Folkeskolen in Denmark 'very clearly facilitates the conditions of the integration of disabled students' (Tetler). In France, 'greater emphasis is being placed on meeting the individual needs of all children', and 'there are plans to introduce changes to the curriculum to allow for greater flexibility' (Armstrong). From Portugal, Da Costa describes the evolution of a 'remedial' room into a 'school resource room' leading to a classical example of reverse takeover: the innovations created there are applied in time in the 'various regular classrooms'.

On the other hand, O'Hanlon recognizes that in the United Kingdom, owing to the preoccupation of schools with 'the requirements of the National Curriculum and trying to ensure that pupils score well in the new testing arrangements, meeting pupils' special needs will be a low priority'. In Greece, 'lately, an intensive evaluation routine has been established, which forces teachers and students to keep up to certain standards' (Lampropoulou and Padeliadou); in this domain, Warnock is not apparently the only British export to the mainland. In The Netherlands (Den Boer) there 'are no common future prospects for those who are politically responsible and those who are affected at school', and 'the permanent excessive demands of the primary school' are leading to 'a growing number of pupils attending a special school'; headteachers of special schools have formed a syndicate to publicize warnings against 'translating the reforms into action too rapidly' – not, an observer might be tempted to think, the most obvious of dangers in the Dutch context. For Randoll the idea of integration is 'in part based on ideologies and Utopian concepts that can hardly be carried out in reality'.

Even in countries where integration is already well developed, or where there is a coherent and comprehensive national plan to promote it, there are causes for concern, although these naturally tend to arise at a different level. For Tetler the doubt is whether the high levels of 'physical integration' in Denmark are 'experienced as meaningful for everyone'. Tetler's fear of the creation of 'a kind of invisible bubble round the students with disabilities' is echoed in Pastor's careful analysis of progress in Spain, where, although 'integration is a way without return', yet, since the authorities have to plan for a determined provision and therefore 'separate integration from other school needs...the organizational principle of integration is opposite to the whole school approach'; at the level of the individual child the Project for Individual Development (PDI) can itself become an isolating factor. Buzzi's critique of the Italian high school recalls similar reservations about equal chances in secondary and upper secondary schooling in the German, French and Spanish chapters, but is particularly severe:

> The high school...remains selective and centralized institutions. They are privileged institutions and almost solely attended (even if less than in the past) by pupils from the middle and upper social classes. They have few links with the social milieu where they are physically located, and have no form of collective decision making process. They have been neglected up to now by the laws of inclusion and mainstreaming of pupils with handicaps.

There is a striking contrast here with the primary and middle schools where integration has forced the recognition 'that it was no longer possible to go on with a school shaped as a mosaic of isolated classes'.

An impediment to progress in integration can be the failure of governments, committed in principle, to support implementation either by means of guidelines or resources. There is a 'lack of direction from the Department of Education' in Ireland, and 'no guidelines regarding integration' (Lynch). The 1985 Law on special education in Greece is not specific on 'how inclusive education ought to be implemented and managed', a lack which 'allows for development towards any possible direction and any possible mistake, too'; at national level 'there is no systematic recording of all the inclusive education projects or initiatives in the Greek school reality' (Lampropoulou and Padeliadou). In spite of the development of regional autonomous communities, on the other hand,

Spain has maintained a clear and strong line of national integration policy; it was perhaps fortunate that two at least of the most prominent regions, Catalonia and the Basque Country, have been forward in promoting inclusive education (Pastor).

Decentralization of administrative and financial policies, whatever its other merits, may militate against the regular implementation of national policy. Germany and the United Kingdom are well known examples of this, and the divergence of practice can be extreme (Randoll, O'Hanlon); variation in levels of integration appears to follow a less obviously political pattern in the United Kingdom than in the Federal Republic. Tetler believes that devolution to counties and municipalities has proved one of the principal barriers to the achievement of consistently effective integration in Denmark. In The Netherlands, fragmentation of a different kind, between the Catholic, Protestant and Public 'pillars', has been a limiting factor; we may deduce that Belgium experiences both this and the effects of regional divisions. In Belgium too the devolution of financial responsibility to schools has led to a decline in the provision for special needs in the regular system (Dens and Hoedemaekers). This will dishearten British readers, but hardly surprise them: O'Hanlon quotes P. Horn for the view that the introduction of the Local Management of Schools (LMS) 'poses much more of a threat to the integration process than any other legislation'.

Yet it must not of course be supposed that decentralization is merely negative in its effects. Lynch regrets the lack of 'local educational administrative structures' in Ireland. In Italy the creation of Local Health Units (USLs) has afforded useful support to a largely centralized educational system, notably in the matter of resources (Buzzi).

Resources are a matter of concern for all our authors. Yet they have surprisingly little to say about technology or even physical accessibility; it is the human factor that counts. Even in the chapter on Germany, where technical developments are so far advanced, Randoll's conclusion is that 'realizing school integration is decisively dependent on the available financial and human resources'. The institution of the National Resource Centre has been an essential element in the implementation of inclusive school policy in Spain, as has the provision of therapeutic and other professional support under the 1985 Royal Decree on Special Education. For Portugal, Da Costa stresses the importance of the institution, as early as the mid-1970s, of local Special Education Teams; also crucial has been the increase in psychological rather than medical influence in the assessment of children. An important factor in the operation of the 'weer samen naar school' (together to school) Act in The Netherlands has been the evolution of special schools into regional resource centres. Progress in Greece is above all impeded by a severe shortage of specialized teachers, therapists and psychologists, amounting to a 'complete lack of support services'.

The role of a 'support teacher' in the regular integrated classroom in Italy has often been reported and is well enough known. What comes out with a new emphasis in these chapters is the importance of the evolution of the role of the 'resource', 'special' or 'support' teacher from that of a specialist giving only a remedial service, by means of withdrawal, to children assessed as having special needs (the 'two per cent' of Warnock), to that of a colleague present in the regular classroom, offering help also to children – Warnock's 20 per cent – with learning difficulties previously unidentified or at least unattended to (Da Costa). In Denmark, success with the integration of more severely impaired children has been achieved by means of teams of teachers including one with a specialized background (Tetler). In ways like this the resource teacher can be seen as supporting not only individual children but the regular teachers themselves too; this in turn leads to a recognition of shared responsibility and so influences ethos and didactics throughout the school (Da Costa, Lynch, Den Boer). Over 20 years ago an Italian ministerial circular called for 'the collective responsibility of the school community in the field of integration' (Buzzi).

Research is recognized as a valid and welcome practical resource. As well, for example, as the Irish studies on attitudes cited by Lynch, Tetler discusses at some length the results of research into the progress of integration in Denmark, Pastor instances research into the effectiveness of support teams in Andalusia, and Lampropoulou and Padeliadou present studies in Thessaloniki on the attitudes of regular teachers. The complaint is not that research is not useful, but that there is not enough of it (Tetler, Lynch, Lampropoulou and Padeliadou). Yet, while research may make a valuable contribution to the identification of good and bad practice and the evaluation of programmes, its usefulness should not amount to a 'plea for making a good idea dependent on empirical findings' (Randoll): 'integration can neither be empirically verified or falsified'. Lampropoulou and Padeliadou agree: the need for 'data based planning' does not 'imply that research data alone could offer a yes or no answer for inclusive education, since the issue has considerable moral relevance'.

The greatest demand of all is for training of professionals, above all of regular teachers – by no means only secondary teachers – who have not during their training learnt 'open or differential forms of teaching'

(Randoll). In in-service training the priority is less for the acquisition of new skills specific to the teaching of children with various categories of handicap than in new ways of managing a whole class and of collaborative ways of working. Training in teamwork is important for specialized support teachers too: 'most would have no previous experience working as a member of an interdisciplinary team in which ideas are shared, joint conclusions drawn and decisions made as a group' (Lynch, cp. Randoll). Specific initial preparation of regular teachers for integrative roles is 'limited and rarely compulsory' in Greece (Lampropoulou and Padeliadou), and not a compulsory component in Ireland (Lynch). For more detail on good initial and in-service training models than can be expected of a book which has to address all the issues of integration, the reader may wish to consult a work devoted to training for special needs in Europe (Mittler and Daunt, 1995).

As well as associating integration with ideology and Utopianism, Randoll, in an important passage, cites research evidence to show that 'children with handicaps feel considerably more integrated emotionally and socially among their equals than in reference groups of children without handicaps', and concludes that 'both school forms have a justified existence and aim at comparable goals using different methods: the integration of people with handicaps into society....One should respect the various forms of schooling...'.

As far as self-esteem goes, Lalkhen and Norwich (1990) had different results; this whole domain may be highly culture-specific. At all events, whereas according special schools respect should be beyond question, any implication that segregated and integrated situations are, in themselves, 'equally good' is a different matter. An attempt to value the two systems equally will have to refute the simple proposition on which the whole structure of school integration in Italy is based, that if the social integration of adults with disabilities is the agreed goal then the social integration of children with disabilities in school is the only defensible means for preparing for it. It would also have to confront the widespread belief in the beneficial effect of integration on children not assessed as having disabilities or specific learning difficulties, above all on those already experiencing or at risk of failure in the regular school (Pastor, Da Costa, Den Boer). And it would of course imply a rejection of the notion of the 'inclusive school' as the dominant focus of educational endeavour from now on, whether or not inclusion is regarded as 'part of the human rights struggle against discrimination' (O'Hanlon, quoting a workshop of the Centre for Studies on Inclusive Education).

Yet Randoll's reservations must be taken seriously. That inclusive education has international authority may not mean much to governments accustomed to giving bland assent in New York, Geneva or Vienna to principles whose consequences they have no intention of implementing, let alone to the United Kingdom which is not even a member of UNESCO. The promotion of the inclusive school as a mid-term goal may be realistic (though only at the level of compulsory education) in the north and south/southwest of the present European Union, that is in Italy, Spain, Portugal and the Nordic countries. The same can hardly be said for Greece, or for a middle belt of Germany, The Netherlands, Belgium and the United Kingdom, and is at the very least doubtful for Austria, France and Ireland.

We need not conclude that the endeavour to promote dialogue and cooperation between all the countries of the Union is based on the assumption of a degree of convergence which does not exist and can only fall apart. Whereas it may be true that 'inclusion has to be total if it is to work' (O'Hanlon, loc. cit.), the same is not so for integration: 'integration and segregation are not mutually exclusive concepts' (O'Hanlon, quoting Hegarty). There may be something here to learn from the approach now being developed in Romania which involves the perception of integration as an all-pervasive concept, relevant for all children with disabilities whatever their situation, but differentiated in response to each reality, something in which all families and professionals, at all levels and sectors of the educational world, have a positive part to play (Diaconescu, *et al.*, 1995). An advantage of this approach is that, in some national situations at least, it is likely to do more for the quality of life of many more children, and much more quickly, than an insistence that only radical individual mainstreaming has any validity.

This will not involve any less responsibility to achieve mainstreaming of that sort whenever it is desired and feasible, but it will involve abandoning, as invidious, the expression 'levels of integration' in favour of 'modes' or 'kinds'. The aspirations of deaf children is of crucial importance here (Den Boer); it is not at all certain that individual mainstreaming is the best way of meeting their needs, which may be better served by means of 'resourced schools' (O'Hanlon, loc. cit.), or by a combination of a specialized unit within a regular school and Individual Education Programmes, as at the Angmering School in England (Daunt, 1991). Much indeed depends on how special classes or units within regular schools are managed, and there are dangers that their contribution to integration may be minimal: in Greece, where 'most students with special needs are supposed to spend at least 80 per cent of their time in their regular education classroom and only go to the resource room for special help...in actual fact, in many cases students stay full-time in the resource room/special class' (Lampropoulou and Padeliadou). In France, the way the Classes d'integration scolaire (CLIS) work is variable, and all are selective, yet at least parents prefer them to special schools (Armstrong, quoting Ballarin).

In the framework of a pervasive policy for integration, the promotion of operational links between special and regular schools and teachers will also be of special value, and the exchange of information on effective models of this will be welcome (Dens and Hoedemaekers; Den Boer).

I believe therefore that the European dialogue has a useful future, indeed an expanding one, to include increasingly the countries of central and eastern Europe not yet members of the Union. And I have no doubt that readers will agree with me that this book makes a substantial and stimulating contribution to this. We need to have a systematic base of data about the children with special needs and the provision for them, something we might well have had already but for the perverse and pusillanimous hostility of national civil servants to the Commission's Handynet project. And there are domains we need to know much more about, such as the upper secondary school, vocational training and the assessment of children – and Scotland.

For such further progress towards a better understanding of each other's situations and towards more effective learning from the common pool of experience, this book has given us both a sound and a challenging basis of information and ideas.

References

Daunt, P. (1991) *Meeting Disability: A European Response*, London: Cassell.

Diaconescu, R., Chis, V. and Daunt, P. (1995) 'Teacher training and the integration of children with special needs: Romanian initiatives', in Mittler, P. and Daunt, P. (eds) *Teacher Education for Special Needs in Europe*, London: Cassell.

Lalkhen, Y. and Norwich, B. (1990) 'The self-concept and self-esteem of adolescents with physical impairments in integrated and special school settings', *European Journal of Special Needs Education*, 5, 1, 1–12.

Mittler, P. and Daunt, P. (1995) *Teacher Education for Special Needs in Europe*, London: Cassell.

CHAPTER 1

The Danish Efforts in Integration

Susan Tetler

The Danish efforts of integration have roots all the way back to the school-policy debate of the 1940s and the 1950s; a debate about the undivided school, a debate about structure, which little by little created a political majority for the opinion that the differentiation of students – after a test in the fifth form – had life-long consequences for the students. That, in other words, the differentiation of students, in fact already determined their future social situation. This debate later split up into two movements, 'the movement for a comprehensive school' and 'the movement for "a school for everyone"', both of them with integration as their main aim.

The comprehensive school

The movement wanted the implementation of the comprehensive school and in a broader sense the integration/inclusion of all ability students, or more correctly, non-segregation.

In 1958 an amendment of the law for the primary school was passed, according to which each school was not allowed to divide the students in the first seven years of schooling, and in 1975 The Primary Act on the Folkeskole, 'in principle', established a comprehensive basic school from the first to the tenth form. In the same period, however, and until about ten years ago, the number of supportive lessons spent on special education increased quite a lot, and these lessons were mainly special arrangements outside the classroom in so-called clinics.

As a Danish politician, Finn Held, then put it: 'We did not suppress the division of school. It is now turning up in another design'. It is exactly this paradoxical incompatibility between, on the one hand, the principal agreement about the aim, 'being willing to integrate even more in general education', and on the other hand, the actual increasing segregation of students and teaching outside the ordinary classroom, which has been the focus of the debate of integration in Denmark. Whereas formerly the school system concentrated on the learning difficulties of the students, attention from now on increasingly turned to the conditions of the school, the conditions which are creating difficulties for the students. This point of view is reflected in the recent legislation. For example, in the Government Notice about special education, where it has been pointed out that 'it lies with every teacher to plan and to carry through his teaching with so much differentiation that to the greatest possible extent it accommodates those differences in learning conditions which the students are having' (Ministry of Education, 1990a).

In 1993 a new law for the primary school was passed. In this law the demand for differentiation in teaching has also been stressed (Lov, 1993).

As the idea of a common norm applied to all students in school now seems to be abandoned, a parallel shift in teacher work becomes possible. Instead of seeking out and naming student learning differences and deficits, teachers from now on shall focus on creating and tailoring the curriculum and teaching so that schooling is in fact working for every student.

The school for everyone

The debate about the comprehensive school in the 1940s and 1950s was mainly about the children who had mild 'special educational needs' and did not do well in school, and this formed the basis of further debate about the schooling of children with more serious and severe learning difficulties.

In the law of 1959, a law about The Care of the Mentally Deficient, the right to education from then on included all children, and as a consequence, the other movement arose – 'The school for everyone'. All children with severe disabilities and handicaps were from now on considered fit for education and with a right to demand a meaningful education. This was an education which strove to comply with the various needs of the students so that all students would be comfortable in a shared teaching environment, and where special arrangements were taking place in a way that made the students as little 'special' as possible. The principle that 'the teaching of handicapped students should be broadened in such a way that the children could be taught in an ordinary school system', was formulated in the Parliamentary Resolution of May 1969, and this resolution at the same time implied four main principles, which became guidelines for local authorities:

1. *The principle of proximity.* This means that assistance to a handicapped child must be offered as close to the child's home and school as possible.
2. *The principle of minimum interference.* This means that a child should not receive any more help than is necessary in order to overcome his or her handicap or its consequences.
3. *The principle of efficiency.* This means that the situations prepared for the child must be worked out in such a way that a handicap can be surmounted, and/or its consequences can be eliminated.
4. *The idea of integration/inclusion.* is based on democratic values: that all human beings are equal and have the same right to full participation, a view which gives everyone the chance to become an important and valued member of the community.

The new ideas were optimistic; they were breaking new ground and had as their foundation principles like integration, normalization and decentralization.

This point of view formed a striking contrast to the former view of segregation. Previously it was seen that a handicap was an individual defect, which could not be helped. Contrary to this the new point of view stressed that a handicap was in some way related to the environment and therefore possible to relieve. According to this perspective, one must act on the basis of a concept of equality, saying that disabled persons – to be set equal – have to be treated differently. As a Danish philosopher, Ole Thyssen puts it:

> To create equality is different from practising equality. Actually you have to discriminate in order to make equal. Equality does not mean uniformity, but rather to be in a position to be educated and to develop. Therefore – equal opportunities to be different. (Thyssen, 1980)

Integration is, seen in that perspective, a step in the direction of diversity and variety.

The new ideas in the 1960s and 1970s were deeply rooted in a socio-economic period of growth and with a consequent optimism, but before the ideas were carried out at all, the material conditions had changed very dramatically – the socio-economic crisis had begun.

At the end of the 1970s, when the principles for the next big educational intervention implemented this reform, 'The decentralisation of the care of handicapped children' had been reduced to only an administrative reform (Lov, 1978). The passing of this law implied that children and young people who so far had been receiving education according to the law of the 'mentally deficient' would in the future receive education according to the law of the primary school.

In January 1980 legislation related to the primary school was modified, which caused a division between the municipalities and the counties. In future the municipality had to take care of the support of students with moderate social and learning difficulties, while the county had to take care of students with more severe disabilities. The then minister of education, Ritt Bjerregard, stressed at the second reading of this reform in Folketinget that it was primarily intended as an administrative reform, meaning that it would not be necessary to decide in the Parliament which way to integrate and to what extent (Bjerregard, 1977). The combined effects of the principles of administrative decentralization and legal normalization meant that the processes of integration and inclusion were determined locally. There is no direct legislation on integration, only guidelines.

By making a point of administrative decentralization, it became more and more a matter of physical integration in so-called 'normal' environments – and with the idea that the social integration was certain to occur. This way of relating to integration implied in Folkeskolen, for example, that the individual integrated students were allocated a number of supportive lessons, but in addition to that they had to adapt to the principles of mainstream/ordinary education. It was seldom a matter of mainstream schools trying to adapt to the needs and backgrounds of these children, as a Danish survey in 1990 showed (Jensen, 1990).

A consequence of this has often been that it has depended exclusively on the individual student and teacher, whether integration would succeed or fail. The role of the school was very seldom referred to with respect to the evaluation of inclusive practices.

The Danish self-image

According to the Helios programme, a resolution concerning 'integration of handicapped children and young people in general systems of education' was passed on 31 May 1990, and it lies with each EU country to intensify its efforts of integration.

According to this resolution the Danish ministry of education has presented a statement about 'The development of the Danish Public

School towards a school for all'. This statement shows great satisfaction with the level of Danish integration – since only a half per cent of the students in the primary and lower secondary school have been educated outside an ordinary school environment (Ministry of Education, 1990b). The conclusion in the Danish statement is that, 'in Denmark we have nearly fulfilled the intentions of the Helios resolution. That is why no initiatives have been taken centrally', and that in Denmark there is a remarkably high level of integration. If you regard integration as a matter of physical integration in the ordinary school there is good reason for the Danish satisfaction, but if, however, the intention is that this physical integration should be experienced as meaningful, too, for everyone, more qualitative research is needed before such confident conclusions can be supported.

Only in a group in which the student or pupil with special educational needs (SEN) or a disability is able to establish mutual social relations, is getting linguistic stimulation and has good opportunities for communication, is able to feel well, secure and accepted, feels that s/he belongs, can the person concerned be said to be integrated. Everything else may, in its utmost consequence, be considered just a school arrangement, or a physical intervention.

Danish research into integration

At the end of the 1980s Danish research into integration was started at the request of LEV (Danish Society for Persons with Learning Disabilities), because of the reports which they had received from a lot of parents telling them about how their individually integrated children seemed to be pushed too hard in their respective classes.

The first part of this research was carried out by Poul Erik Jensen, of The Danish Institute for Educational Research, and is a description of the kind and the extent of educational integration for all children with severe learning disabilities who were enrolled in ordinary classes in the school year 1987/88 (Jensen, 1990b).

The second and third part of this research give a more general picture of whether teachers, other groups of staff and parents felt that Folkeskolen was able to teach students with severe learning disabilities. In the second part, Ole Varming and Ole Eistrup Rasmussen from The Royal Danish School of Educational Studies focus on situations in school, and they do this on the basis of inquiries and interviews with teachers, social educators, headteachers, school psychologists and educational advisers (Varming and Rasmussen, 1990). In the third part, which also contains interviews, Gugu Kristoffersen tries to convey the experiences of the parents concerning their lives with a child with a disability (Kristoffersen, 1990).

The first part shows that the number of students who are recorded as students with severe learning disabilities (2,546) has been constant. Seventy per cent of them have been taught in county special schools, and only 8 per cent have been individually integrated in the ordinary classes in Folkeskolen. It is with those 8 per cent that the research is concerned. It is a common and distinct feature of the process of integration that it falls apart as the students grow older, and the number of students in mainstream education is reduced suddenly after the seventh form. Poul Erik Jensen, who has prepared the results, suggests that a more suitable school solution is found after the seventh form, partly because of the high level of abstraction expected in lessons after the seventh form, and partly because of the social neglect of students by their classmates. The tendency is clearly that the child with a disability starts his/her earlier school years in an educationally integrated situation, which little by little becomes more isolated.

The research points to the basic question of whether the integrated students are present in the classes they are supposed to be taught with. The results indicate that most of the individually integrated students have been wholly or partly segregated from several of the subjects taught in the school. Many students are excluded from certain subjects, and a great number have only a few lessons with their classmates, and there are often lessons where the work is individually planned, and which focus on skills training.

In the second part of the research the interviews indicate that the process of integration in the schools often has an accidental character. Not all schools, for example, have followed a certain strategy or a school policy or plan. It appears as if most of the practical work of including the student, which actually ought to be the joint responsibility of the school, has been left up to individual teachers. This implies that individual teachers or the teacher-team have to initiate or assume the responsibility that their students are to be included in the activities of the school. An another important conclusion which can be drawn from this research has to do with the internal and external relations of cooperation, which according to the teachers interviewed are of a highly varied quality. While the teachers express themselves positively about the internal cooperation taking place between the teachers in a class, they express discontent in relation to the other teachers in the school, the school psychologist, the counselling service, the administrators and the staff of the youth centres. Ole Varming and Ole Eistrup conclude that the teachers miss much-needed support from the psychologists, and in general it is characteristic that the further you move from the classroom, the less cooperation you receive and it is seen to be of poorer quality.

In the third part of the research, half of the parents said that schoolmates did not visit their disabled classmates in their homes, nor did the child with a disability have any local playmates. As few of the parents mentioned teasing, it appears that children with a disability are not being teased in the school. The students with disabilities are able to make relationships within the school, but those relationships seem not to develop into friendships outside of school. Also, many of the parents said that they don't feel that they have had any real choice regarding the choice of school for their child with a disability (Kristoffersen, 1990). Some parents got the school they wanted, for others it was the only choice, but very many found it important that it was a small-sized local school.

There appears to be no homogeneous procedure in municipalities and counties when a decision is being made about where and when the child is going to start school. Apparently it depends on where the parents live. The parents express a wish for a broad range of proposals; they want both/and, not either/or. What is good at one moment may not to be good at another. The message is one of relativity and the need to constantly check on the child's educational needs which change from year to year (ibid.)

A decentralized strategy of development

There is no doubt that in Denmark we have had the best intentions in regard to integration. Why then have even the best intentions been so difficult to carry through? One of the explanations, I think, is that since 1969 we have had a socially formulated ambition of integrating students with disabilities, but the central administration has not yet started a programme of implementation in order to carry out the efforts of integration. Instead, it has been left to the municipalities; in fact, it has often been left to the individual teacher to start and carry out projects to include students in their classrooms and schools.

There are indeed some municipalities (Rodovre, Esbjerg, Gladsaxe and Nakskov) which, on the basis of more long-sighted and conscious planning, have tried to integrate their students with disabilities into the Folkeskolen, but otherwise it is characteristic that the integration projects have been initiated, carried out and evaluated by individual teachers or teacher-teams. Often the projects have existed as ‘small islands’ in the schools, and the experiences have little chance of spreading in a wider circle to the entire school. No national or regional networks have been established for mutual support, inspiration and, not least, systematic preparation or evaluation of the experiences. Therefore the ideas and the experiences have passed away little by little, and, perhaps after a while and independent of the earlier experiences, have arisen again in quite a different place in Denmark. In this way the experiences have only been repeated, instead of being the dynamic starting points for further developments in inclusive education. This very decentralized strategy of development seems not to be ideal, when the aim is to change practice so radically – from segregation to integration.

Special educational projects of development

In 1987 a general development of the primary school was one of the most important items on the agenda of Parliament. A Programme of Development was passed, the main aim of which was to reform the framework and the curriculum of the school. For that purpose, 100 million kroner were set aside yearly for a period of four years (Ministry of Education, 1987).

In the first two years of this programme – 1988 and 1989 – only ten projects of integration/inclusion were started, and it is characteristic that in all ten projects it was a matter of group integration; more precisely they are about teaching a special class with an ordinary class to a greater or smaller extent, with varying amounts of curriculum inclusion. In seven of the projects the ordinary class and the special class are placed in the same school, while the other three have established teamwork between neighbouring schools – a special school and an ordinary school. Only in one case, in Madeskovskolen in Nakskov, is it a matter of complete and total integration; that means that all students follow the same schedule, have the same classrooms and the same teachers. In the other projects, integration is rather fragmentary (Hatt and Christensen, 1993).

So only to a limited extent have attempts at integration been made. The inclusion of students takes place for short periods, partly when the students in the class are working with certain themes, or in certain subjects, for two to four lessons weekly. Altogether there is agreement between the reality the research is reflecting, and the reality of which the research of Poul Erik Jensen is a quantified expression.

In these projects, there is an overall tendency primarily to integrate students into craft, art and music subjects, and as early as possible. In three of the projects, students in the sixth form have been integrated, while the other projects are about efforts of integration in the second or third form. The idea of integration proves not to be a too-ambitious Utopia, if we examine the evidence of the project from Madeskovskoien in Nakskov (ibid.). The project was started in the 1983, with a first-form special class combining teaching with an ordinary/mainstream first-form class. In 1985 the project was given the status of a pilot experiment under Folkeskolen's Development Board and later became a part of the Programme of Development. The project was finished in 1992 after nine years of joint schooling. The educational practice of this project is based on the understanding that a handicap is relative and, therefore, among other things, determined by local planning and implementation of education. Therefore the teachers strove to take each child as a starting point when planning and organizing their education, so that all students could develop their real competencies and their possibilities for educational achievement. The building stones in this project have been:

- the organization of the education is, regarding subjects and lessons, undivided and unified;
- alternation between periods of courses with a differentiated curriculum connected specifically to the subjects, and periods of themes, whose curriculum often cuts across the subject divisions (interdisciplinary teaching);
- workshops, which are based on the experiences of the students and on autonomy;
- daily class meetings and conflict resolution;
- organization of the two classrooms to make various activities for various groups possible at the same time.

The principles and conditions of the project have been:

- the special class was taught with an ordinary class of the same age;
- the average size of the class was a maximum of 20 students, of whom three to four students belonged to the special class. There were three to four students in the ordinary class too who had some minor learning difficulties;
- the teacher-team consisted of three teachers, one of whom had a specialized educational background;
- the timetabling and organization of lessons made it possible for two teachers to be present at the same time;
- both the students of the special class and the students of the ordinary

class followed the curriculum, approved by the municipality of Nakskov.

What is remarkable about this project is that it has, all throughout the nine years of schooling, succeeded in creating a school life which has included both students with disabilities and mainstream students. In a survey of inquiry, midway in the seventh form, by far the greater part of the so-called 'normal' students said that the peer relationships and companionship in this class were good, while most of the students with SEN considered they were really good (Frey, 1992).

In general the students with SEN in this survey expressed a very positive attitude to schooling, which is remarkable because Poul Erik Jensen, in the first part of his research, could demonstrate that before the integration project many individually integrated students were segregated from Folkeskolen.

Danish tendencies in integration up to now

The Danish psychologist Ivy Schousboe makes an attempt to distinguish between four different kinds of integration on the basis of their different aims. On the one hand, she sees a cooperative kind of integration. The characteristic feature of which is that the established social unit and the teacher/s cooperate on deciding aims for the integration, because it has not been decided in advance what to do about the diversity of the person's educational needs in an integrated context (Shousboe, 1989).

In the other three kinds of integration the aim has, on the contrary, been decided by the established social unit before integration takes place. In the assimilation model of integration, the aim is that the student with SEN gives up and gets rid of his/her diversity and becomes like the others, whereas in a fragmentary integration, the aim is that the student with SEN is partly assimilated and partly keeps his/her diversity.

The fourth kind of integration is described as formal, the characteristic feature of which is diffuse goals: there will be integration, but no specific considerations have been developed with reference to whom, what, how and why to integrate.

I am of the opinion that it is the cooperative kind of integration which is worth striving for. In particular, it is important for me to stress that integration is a process of interaction, where the participants have the attitude that changes have to take place not only in the person, whom they seek to integrate, but also in the integrating social unit. Seen in a social perspective, the crucial question then is not whether the society is willing to strive for integration, but that it is – on what basis and in which form? Therefore, I agree with the Swede Marten Soder, when he says that an abstract question about whether you are for or against integration is absurd, as the answer always depends on the concrete and available possibilities (Soder, 1990). That is what every discussion about, integration has to be about because only then can you decide whether the efforts of integration will be linked to the adaptation and conformity of the individual, or whether there is an opportunity for the person to develop in a diverse and individual manner.

In spite of the slender research material available in Denmark, I will try to draw a picture of the Danish efforts in integration up to now, and this I will do on the basis of the model of the four kinds of integration:

1. The cooperative kind of integration seems to be the exception.
2. The integration of a single student in an ordinary class often seems to have assimilation features.
3. The integration of a group of students in an ordinary class is, on the contrary, most often fragmentary. This implies that general/mainstream education will not be changed as a result of a single student with SEN or disabilities being integrated. Only when a large group of students with disabilities are being integrated is it found necessary to change the curriculum and the organization of the school. In return, a group of students with disabilities are taught with the ordinary class for only a short period.
4. Politicians and administrators of the Danish municipalities seem to react formally to the question about integration, rather than considering the real context. On the one hand they believe that integration *per se* is desirable, but on the other hand there is a lack of well-defined goals, there is a lack of analyses of the local capacity of integration, and finally, they have not decided any plans of implementation about how to further the quality of integration of students with a disability.

If my conclusion is true, this is unfortunate, because the then Minister of Education, Bertel Haarder, in his answer to Folketinget, renounces the responsibility for the development of a 'school for everyone' – and instead delegates the responsibility to the same municipalities (Haarder, 1992).

A forward-looking perspective

Even if the efforts of integration up to now in Denmark still, generally, leave much to be desired, I see no reason to throw out the baby with the bath water. Quite the reverse, I think the aim of integration is still worth striving for, but then, in return, I find it necessary to start research which is not only content with noting what reality looks like, but is also attempting to analyse what room there seems to be for the real, active integration processes.

In the debate on integration up to now, the term has often been used in a slogan-like manner, As a result it is simplified and generalized, and covers a varied and complex educational context. The Norwegian Trygve Lie has pointed out that integration from a special education point of view can be looked upon as a process of interaction, where participants with different backgrounds are acting without fear of showing or losing identity (Lie, 1970). In this way the term marks both a goal and a process – a complex process of interaction with very idealistic goals. I therefore find it necessary to split up this complex process of interaction into well-defined parts of the process. In this way the limits and fractured surfaces of the efforts of integration up to now and in the future will be more distinct. Differentiating the integration processes and looking at them on their different levels could also facilitate the opportunity to carry through more concrete and well-defined initiatives.

The German psychologist Heimuth Reiser and his research team see the processes of integration in three German kindergartens as taking place on four levels: the level of society, the level of institution, the level of interaction and finally the level of the individual (Reiser *et al.*, 1987).

They understand the process of integration as the processes by which you are coming to an agreement – with yourself and/or each other. Coming to an agreement is not calling for homogeneous interpretations, aims or ways of conduct, but is rather calling for a readiness to let the positions of the others count as equal, without considering these or your own position as different. This implies giving up pursuing what is different – in order to discover the collective possibilities by accepting what is different.

The level of the individual is the basis of all the following levels; as far as 'coming to an agreement' on the other levels this only succeeds if you have come to an agreement with yourself.

The level of interaction is the factual basis for all the processes of integration and in a way the condition of the level of the individual, too, because it is on that level you have the possibility of having relationships with others.

On *the level of the institution,* the issue is how to initiate and carry

through the process of integration. It is the administrative basis of integration, which is going to remain ineffective without the process of integration on the level of the individual and the level of interaction.
The *level of society* is the normative/social basis for the process of integration.

I am concerned with primary and lower secondary schools in Denmark. I have to add a further level: a level on which the integrating teaching takes place. Because of the fact that education in Denmark is to a large extent decentralized, a level of the local community is necessary as level six. The processes of integration – taking place on those six levels – have to be analysed and evaluated in order to identify the factors which seem to hinder or facilitate their development. In that way I see a good opportunity for further qualifying the local efforts in integration.

A concept of an integrated education

From a pragmatic point of view it is not relevant to ask whether the child with a disability can join mainstream education, but it is instead relevant to ask how the circumstances in the school can be arranged in a way that make the educational development of each child possible. From this point of view it is important to throw light on the curriculum and the organization of schools.

Danish as well as Swedish research demonstrates that the integration of children with disabilities does not automatically result in integrating activities in the schools (Varming and Jensen, 1989). On the contrary, it looks as if parallel activities are often developed, which may be general classroom activities up to now, or more specific subject-based activities which are usually separated from the former. American researchers too, for example Dianne Ferguson, confirm the phenomenon that children who are integrated often become 'bubble kids', where they stay within a kind of capsule in the education system (Ferguson, 1992).

Inclusive teaching is much more than the introduction of supportive arrangements carried out by a special teacher, while the other teaching in the classroom remains unchanged. Seen against that background it becomes important to identify the incidents and the events which seem to create invisible bubbles around the students with disabilities, and thus hinder real inclusion in the classroom.

It is a goal in itself to explore how regular/mainstream education and special education activities can fuse into a combined form of integrating practice which is able to contain a sense of community, where the ideal is the recognition of student diversity, and where that recognition of the diversity as well as the fellowship of the group does itself justice. Such a practice cannot arise by itself, but is like any other educational work: 'hard work'. It is exactly a development of these didactic and methodical aspects of an inclusive education which has been the primary concern of the Nakskov project.

An analysis of these integrating processes points out that differentiating, thematic and interdisciplinary organization of the curriculum, organization in workshops, project work, flexible structuring of time and a contributory influence of students are able to form some of the basic building blocks in the concept of integrating education (Tetler, 1990). Integration has to be seen in proportion to the possibilities which are present or, just as important, may become present. If, however, the efforts of integration prove successful, it is necessary to look at them as a joint concern of the school, and not like now, where special education practice often appear as 'a school within the school'.

When now I look rather optimistically at the efforts of integration, it is because in Denmark we are moving into a phase where to a larger extent there is a focus on the content of the integrational processes in Folkeskolen and a striving to develop inclusive principles and teaching methods. The differentiation of students within the curriculum can be seen as one of these principles.

From August 1994 The Act of Folkeskolen is to be implemented. It is a reform which very clearly facilitates the conditions of the integration of students with disabilities (Lov, 1993), as a result of which the Danish efforts in integration could well be characterized as 'inclusive schooling' or as we say in Denmark, 'a school for everyone'.

We, too, have little by little made good progress through good experiences concerning team teaching, and we see it as an advantage that there is no barrier between the general teachers and the special teachers. A special teacher in Denmark has been trained as a generalist as well as a specialist. That is because the training for special teachers takes place after initial teacher training. Thus we have been given an opportunity to break down the divide between the general/mainstream teacher and the special teacher which I have seen act as an obstacle in both German and American integration projects. I therefore see a potential for the development of integrating processes in Folkeskolen; however, there are also very strong and élitist interests in school and society, who are striving for quite different goals. How far we can get with the goal of inclusion is not only a question of development and research, but also a question of education and, in the last resort depends on the goals of society.

References

Bjerregaard, R. (1977), i: *Folketingstidende 1977–78*, bind 7, Spaite 11240.

Ferguson, D. (1992) m.fl, *Figuring Out what to do with grownups: How teachers make Inclusion work for students with disabilities*, Jash, Vol. 17, no. 4, 218–26

Frey, B, m.fi. (1992), *Specialundervisningens mange ansigter*, DPI, Copenhagen.

Haarder, B. (1992), *Svar pa Sporgsmal*, 148 af 1 1 maj.

Hatt and Christensen (1993), *lntegreret undervisning, Et bud pci skolen for alle. Madeskovskolen*, Nakskov.7 Arsrapporter fra 1986–92.

Jensen, P.E. (1990) *'§ 1 9 stk. 2-elevers integration'*, Foriaget Skolepsykoiogi.

Kristoffersen, G. (1990), *Skolen og livet*, Foriaget Skoiepsykoiogi.

Lie, T. (1970), *Tanker omkring visse internationals stromninger i specialundervisningen*. S.A.-paedagogen nr. 3.

Lov af 8. juni 1978, Parliament Copenhagen.

Lov om folkeskoie (1993), vedtaget d. 23. juni, Copenhagen.

Ministry of Education (1987) *Udvikiingsprogram for folkeskoien og skoien som lokalt kulturcenter*, vedtaget d. 26 maj, Copenhagen.

Ministry of Education (1990a), *Bekendtgorelse* nr. 537 af 16 juli, Copenhagen.

Ministry of Education (1990b), *Undervisningsministeriets redegorelse*, til Folketinget, Copenhagen.

Reiser, Kiein, Kreie and Kron (1987), *Integrative Prozessen in integrativen Kindergartengruppen*, Juvena, Munchen.

Schousboe, I. (1989), *Integrationsformer*, Udkast nr. 1.

Soder, M. (1990), *Ved en forelaesning pa Danmarks Laererhojskoie* d. 18 sept, Copenhagen.

Tetler, S. (1990) *Integrative processer i folkeskolen. En analyse af den intenderede, den faktiske og den mulige praksis*, DLH Copenhagen.

Thyssen, O. (1980), *Fhhed og Lighed,* in, Demokrati/Krise og utopi – Gyldendal.

Varming and Jensen (1989), § 19 stk. 2 – elevers integration, *Foriaget Skoirpsykoiogi 1989 Hill & Rabe Den onda cirkeln – och den goda*, paper for konferencen om Barn med psykisk utveck-lingsstorning i forskolan. Stockholm, jan.

Varming, O. and Rasmussen, O. E. (1990) *lntegrationens born*, Foriaget Skoiepsykoiogi.

CHAPTER 2

Special Education in France: 'Passé Historic' *or* 'Futur Simple'

Felicity Armstrong

The French education system in all its complexity is the legacy of a number of different historic strands and events. The most important of these have their roots in the French revolution of 1789 and in the Paris Commune of 1871. Such a statement suggests perhaps a smooth and even line of historic development, which can be traced from particular events and along certain rational, expected pathways. But there have been other, separate routes running alongside and sometimes crossing the formal legislative ones relating to education. This chapter will examine some of the issues arising out of the complex and diverse systems which have grown up to accommodate children and young people with disabilities and difficulties in learning.

The principles of liberty, equality and fraternity which emerged during the French Revolution have found expression in the education system and continue to be asserted with a startling energy when they appear to be threatened. Laying an historical claim to these principles is the highly centralized state apparatus which includes the state education system established in the Napoleonic era and after. This system was based on a national curriculum and centrally-generated directives on planning and pedagogy.

Historically, as in many other European countries, provision for children and young people with disabilities and learning difficulties has by and large developed outside the state education system and has not traditionally been included in its frame of reference. The structures and institutions which have grown up separately from the educational apparatus have often been seen as having a therapeutic, social or medical purpose rather than a primarily educational one. In addition, although state schools are ostensibly 'for everybody', it is only recently that the question of how to meet the needs of individual pupils in ordinary schools has become the focus of national debate in education. Yet it is still generally accepted that some young people will continue to be excluded from ordinary schools.

Like everywhere else, the economic, social and cultural realities of the late twentieth century have given rise to new preoccupations and challenges and a rejigging of old ones. The values, structures and practices which accompanied other periods are being constantly questioned and shaken up in response to these challenges. The concept of the rights of all groups to be fully included in society and to enjoy a rich and fulfilled life is in theory largely unchallenged. The right of disabled children and young people to be fully included in ordinary schools has been laid down in legislation, but such rights are often found to be at odds with the structures and practices already deeply rooted in society. This chapter looks at the issues which arise out of these contests.

The education system

Although compulsory schooling does not begin until a child is 6 years old, over 99 per cent of 3-year-olds attend nursery school (écoles maternelles) in France and many start at the age of 2. Compulsory primary education was introduced in 1882 and later extended to the secondary stage. One of the fundamental principles of state education from its inception has been its secularism, still vehemently defended 150 years later. Prior to the introduction of compulsory state education, primary schools had generally been under the control of the Catholic church (*The Guardian* 29 July 1994, p.9). Underlying this principle was another still more fundamental one – that of inclusion. No child should be excluded on the grounds of religion, gender or nationality.

The primary phase of education lasts for five years until the age of 11 when pupils transfer to the 'college' for four years. Up to this stage all pupils in ordinary schools follow a common national curriculum, but after the second year at the college a process of selection takes place and pupils are channelled along different routes. Those who are regarded as capable of following an academic route are streamed into a 'general' academic direction. Others are allocated to classes which will prepare them for transfer to the *lycée professionnel* which, as well as providing basic and 'remedial' education, introduces students to various vocational professions such as painting and decorating, pastry cooking, plumbing, hairdressing, etc. In effect, this means that some young people are having to choose their future career path at the age of 14, thus reducing their opportunities and restricting flexibility on the labour market at a time when unemployment is running at 12.4 per cent generally, and at an even higher rate among young people. Pupils staying on at school after the statutory leaving age of 16, transfer to either a lycée generale or a lycée professionnel. At the former, they study for the traditional academic baccalaureat or the 'technology' baccalaureate; at the latter they take the vocational baccalaureate, the CAP, or the less prestigious basic *brevet d'études professionelles* (the BEP). The 'New Contract For Schools' put forward in July 1994 proposes to introduce greater flexibility between the different streams in secondary education so that students can change course with greater ease.

Special education

The following section describes the separate development of special provision and the state education system and how this has been encouraged by the growth of institutions outside the education system and by the nature of the curriculum and organization within that system. For these reasons only major structural and curricular changes and a change of ethos will make the inclusion of all pupils in one system possible.

It would be hard to establish a precise date in French history as a marker for the beginnings of 'special education'. No doubt, formal and informal arrangements and practices to help and support those with disabilities have been in operation in different forms for hundreds – even thousands – of years. Social responses to disability and learning difficulties have focused on finding a 'solution' to problems perceived as arising out of differences between individuals. In all European countries such responses have included the segregation of some people from the rest of society. This is still the case and it is against this heavy legacy that the struggle for inclusion takes place. For the purposes of this section I shall take 1793 as the symbolic date for my starting point, which was the year in which Doctor Philippe Pinel was granted permission from the Commune of Paris to release 89 'lunatics' from their shackles.

> Up until this time, the insane were herded together. with convicts and criminals. In chains, they coexisted on bedding of damp straw in darkened,

> airless prison cells. For the first time, the insane became 'the sick' who deserved treatment and care and this change in attitude marked the growth of modern psychiatry which was to spread throughout Europe. (Bouissou, 1967)

Their status changed from that of being totally excluded and reviled, to being segregated, 'treated' and deemed worthy of help.

This is an important landmark in the history of provision for children and young people with psychiatric or learning difficulties because it marked a move away from a purely custodial model towards a medical model of care and treatment which has an important presence in the French system today. A further legacy of the work of Pinel and others is the practice of diagnosing and categorizing conditions and disabilities (commonly referred to as 'nosologie' in the eighteenth century) and the matching of these to available provision. The degree to which categorization determines educational placement varies from region to region and between institutions.

A second development in the history of special education in France was the opening of schools for the deaf and the blind in the eighteenth century. These were often provided by religious institutions; Abbe de l'epée set up a school for the 'deaf-mute' and Valentin Hauy opened an institution for blind children during this period. Other similar institutions followed. There is little evidence that there was provision for children with severe physical or learning difficulties during this period.

During the late nineteenth century there was a growth of interest in psychology and psychoanalysis, but at this stage little attention was paid to social factors which might contribute to the development of the child. The end of the nineteenth century saw the growth in provision for children in psychiatric hospitals where they received treatment for their conditions but were generally regarded as 'ineducable'.

In 1909 a law was passed enabling the setting up through local initiatives of 'improvement classes' (*classes de perfectionnement*) for children with learning difficulties (*les enfants handicapées mentaux*) attached to ordinary elementary schools for pupils between the ages of 6–14. In reality such classes contained a broad diversity of pupils, including those with physical and sensory disabilities, those with learning difficulties and others with emotional and behavioural difficulties. The reason for this was not because there were accepted policies concerning integration or inclusion but because there were no easily accessible alternatives for pupils with a wide range of difficulties (Lantier, *et al.*, 1994).

The 1950s to 1980s

During the period between 1950 and 1970, a large network of 'establishments' began to grow up in response to pressure from parents and in a favourable economic climate in which the government could afford to fund such expansion. Associated with the growth of this system of special provision was the demand for preventative measures and the right to an education in contrast to medical treatment and therapy. Greater attention was paid to the social needs of children and young people with disabilities and learning difficulties and their right to be included in the community was acknowledged. Although the network of '*medico-educatif*' establishments grew up outside the state education system, by 1975 it had become widely accepted that such a system effectively segregated many young people from the rest of the community.

In June 1975, in response to changing attitudes and pressure from parents, the *Loi d'orientation en Faveur des Personnes Handicapes* was passed. This law asserted the right of access to social integration of all children, young people and adults with physical, sensory or mental disabilities. In addition, it laid down the right to education, training, work and financial support and outlined the structural and procedural changes which would implement and facilitate increased participation of children and young people in ordinary schools. The law stated that children should, where possible, be admitted to ordinary schools 'in spite of their handicap'.

The 1975 law, which acknowledged the principle of inclusion, was followed by government circulars (1983, 1985) with guidelines on the mechanisms through which integration should take place. In spite of the legislation and a common acceptance of the principles which underlay it, the continued existence of a large and complex network of special schools and institutions, together with the nature of the curriculum in ordinary schools acted as a break on the inclusion of pupils with disabilities and learning difficulties in mainstream state education.

The Loi Jospin

The Law of Orientation 1989 (The '*Loi Jospin*') introduced further changes relating to other aspects of the education system as a whole and to ways in which the needs of individual pupils in primary schools might be met, as well as introducing changes in teacher education. Again, the Act has been followed by a number of government circulars which have elaborated on various aspects of the legislation. The *Loi Jospin* reiterated the importance of educational integration as part of a process of inclusion in society and invited the services provided by the Ministry for Health to participate in this process. Subsequent circulars stipulated structural and pedagogical changes which would facilitate integration. The circulars recognize the diverse needs of pupils and the complex relationship which exists between the education system and structures which are controlled by the Ministry of Health. In addition, some specialist establishments are controlled by the Ministry of Education. The task of breaking down the barriers and renegotiating long-held territories and power bases is not an easy one.

One of the most important principles underlying the *Loi Jospin* was the importance of opening up the education system to a greater number of children and young people and to make progress within it more accessible. Linked to this principle was a determination to improve the quality of teaching and learning for all pupils The declared objective of 80 per cent of school leavers attaining the baccalaureate by the year 2,000 and the remaining 20 per cent achieving the CAP has become a focal point for reform and change in education.

It was recognized that to achieve this target, changes would have to take place in schools so that the needs of all pupils could be addressed. The various circulars which have followed the introduction of this law have introduced a number of important changes, especially in primary schools.

Specialist provision and change in ordinary schools

Provision in, or attached to, ordinary schools for pupils who have disabilities or experience difficulties in learning is remarkably diverse, reflecting both 'the new' and 'the old'. Structures established nearly a century ago coexist with new models introduced since 1989.

As a result of legislation following the *Loi Jospin*, 'integration classes', known as *Classes d'integration scolaire* (CLIS), have been established which are attached to ordinary schools to facilitate the inclusion of pupils with visual, hearing and physical disabilities and those who experience difficulties in learning. The form that these classes take and their relationship with mainstream classes within the ordinary school varies according to the philosophy of the school, the degree of difficulty experienced by the pupils and the personal work style of the teachers. Much depends on the degree to which specialist teachers and class teachers feel they can share their expertise and experience, and the degree to which pupils are truly included in the life of the school is uneven. The CLIS do not provide for all pupils who experience difficulties.

> These classes in certain schools provide in a differentiated way for those handicapped pupils who can benefit from being in an ordinary school and from receiving an education adapted to meet their needs taking into account their age and the nature and degree of their handicap. The objective of the CLIS is to allow pupils to follow, either entirely or partially, an ordinary path. (Ballarin, 1994)

However, the *Classes d'integration scolaire* are selective. Not all children with disabilities or difficulties in learning can expect to find a place.

> The CLIS is a class for the handicapped, but admission is conditional. Not all mental handicap falls within the province of the CLIS. This must be clearly explained to parents who have a tendency to prefer their child to be offered a place in a *Classe d'integration scolaire* than in a specialist centre, because the education of the young handicapped person in an (ordinary) elementary school is always considered preferable to placement in a special school. However, in spite of their specialisation, the role of the CLIS is limited. They are not appropriate for all those with learning difficulties (*'les deficients intellectuals'*). They are there to provide an education which is adapted for those who can benefit from it. (Ballarin, op.cit., p.9)

In addition to the CLIS, there are also the '*classes a effectif reduit*' ('classes of reduced size'), more popularly known as '*classes d'adaptation fermée*' ('closed adaptation classes') and the '*regroupement d'adaptation*' or '*classes d'adaptation ouverte*' ('open adaptation classes'). The first of these are classes which have no more than 15 pupils and are for those children entering primary school who experience general difficulties in learning. The purpose of these classes is to give each pupil individual help while following the same curriculum as the other children, in order to enable them to join an ordinary class as quickly as possible. The second type are 'closed' because the child belongs to this class and does not join the ordinary class. These classes are gradually being replaced by other approaches such as the differentiation of curriculum content and delivery. The 'open adaptation classes' are there to support pupils who are experiencing difficulties in particular areas of learning such as reading. Pupils join these classes at particular times in the week for help in these areas. In rural areas these 'open adaptation classes' are peripatetic and serve a number of schools in a particular geographical area. In effect, specialist staff visit different schools on different days of the week.

In addition, there are still *Classes de perfectionnement* (improvement classes) which were first introduced in 1909. These may be individual classes attached to ordinary schools, but occasionally a whole school is made up of these 'improvement classes'. It is expected that these classes will gradually be replaced by the CLIS.

There are also a number of children who are integrated into ordinary schools and classes on a full- or part-time basis and receive specialist support from a variety of agencies. This model of integration is rather different from those in which the child receives most of his or her teaching from a specialist teacher, often in a special class attached to an ordinary class. *L'integration individuelle* (individual integration) is described as 'concerning the admission into an ordinary class with an ordinary teacher without specialist training...and (with the purpose of) assuring (the handicapped pupils) a life as similar to those of their peers as possible' (Ballarin, 1994, p.6).

It is difficult to gather statistics on the number of pupils receiving help within each model of provision. At what point, for example, is a children in a CLIS and at what point can they be considered a full member of an ordinary class? The problem becomes more acute when 'integration' is discussed. Not only are there important differences within one model of provision according to area, and local conditions and ethos, but the way in which the term 'integration' is used varies widely.

Secondary provision

When pupils transfer to the college and start the secondary phase of their education, the range of structures and provision for those with disabilities or learning difficulties becomes less diverse. As a result, a number of pupils transfer to special schools, some of which may not be under the control of the Ministry of Education. Those who remain in the system but for whom an ordinary education is not considered appropriate, attend the *sections d'education specialisée* – 'specialist education sections'. These are separate groups of classes attached to colleges and follow the same pattern of school day but with a different curriculum. They were established in 1966 originally for pupils with 'slight intellectual deficiency' aged 12–16 whose IQs were measured as falling between 65 and 80 points with no other major difficulties. In practice, many young people attending the SES are there because of disruptive behaviour in school and difficulties which have arisen in association with behavioural difficulties.

Pupils follow a curriculum based largely on basic skills and practical training for manual work. Since the *Loi Jospin* in 1989, the SES have been authorized to extend their provision for young people up to the age of 18 or 19 for the purposes of offering them courses leading to accreditation. A reduction in the official statistics for youth unemployment is a by-product of this.

The failure to provide a diversity of provision at secondary level within the education system means that the number of young people in segregated special institutions increases dramatically at around the age when pupils would ordinarily transfer to a college. According to OECD figures (Table 2.1) this is in sharp contrast to many other countries.

Table 2.1 Percentage of children in special school by level of schooling

Country	*Pre-school*	*Primary*	*Secondary*
Belgium	0.55	3.90	3.40
Finland	n/a	6.21	3.70
France	0.3	2.00	3.70
Greece	0.10	1.40	0.12
Ireland	n/a	1.00	0.90
Japan	n/a	0.33	0.44
Netherlands	0.71	5.64	2.48
Norway	n/a	0.21	0.38
Spain	0.50	0.90	0.20

n/a = not available

Special schools

There are still a small number of *Les écoles de plein air* ('Open-air schools') which became popular in the 1930s. They are controlled by the Ministry of Education and the children, who usually have some form of physical disability, follow the same curriculum as other schools. These schools, which may be residential or non-residential, are for children for whom an education away from the inner city is deemed beneficial.

Special schools and institutions outside the state education system

Provision for children and young people with disabilities and difficulties in learning who do not come under the umbrella of the Ministry for Education is controlled by a variety of bodies. Many institutions have more in common with a medical setting than an educational one. There are still a number of establishments which were set up as a response to particular disabilities or medical conditions. Examples of this kind of setting are the *atriums, preventoriums* and *institute helio-marins* which were set up to provide children with both treatment for tuberculosis and an education. Admission to these establishment is made through medical prescription and discussion with all those concerned with the child's health and education.

Les hopitaux de jour ('Day hospitals')

These hospitals are for children and adults with psychiatric problems and are non-residential. They do not themselves provide any schooling, but children may attend a local school on a part-time basis.

Les maisons d'enfants ('children's homes')

These are residential and may provide schooling themselves or children may attend local schools. Teachers who work in these settings may be employed by the Ministry of Education or directly by the institutions themselves.

There are two categories of *maison d'enfants*. The *maison d'enfants à caractre sanitaire* receives children who experience a wide range of difficulties and include those who are identified as needing a period of time in a healthy environment with good nourishment, as well as children who are recovering from an operation or illness and children who are seen as physically fragile and who need 'building up'. The *maisons d'enfants à caractere specialise* are for children who need treatment for a particular medical condition (asthma, epilepsy, respiratory conditions, diabetes, etc.).

Admission to both these is made through a medical prescription and after agreement with the social security office, which will meet the costs of this provision (Ballarin, 1994).

Children with severe learning difficulties and disabilities are usually placed in a centre referred to as a *hebergement* ('shelter') where they receive medical treatment and therapy. Usually teachers are not employed in these settings. When young people reach adulthood they usually transfer to a *maison d'accueil specialisée* (MAS). There is a serious shortage of places in these settings, and many young people and adults do not find a place. Children and young people with visual or hearing impairment usually attend a *centre pour deficients sensoriels* (centre for sensory impairment) where they receive specialist teaching by teachers who have received training in visual or hearing impairment.

Many young people with learning difficulties attend *les institute medico-educatifs* (medical-educational centres) or an *external medico-professionel* (non-residential medical training centres). These institutions are run by the local authority and the Ministry for Health and Social Affairs. Teachers may well be employed by the Ministry for Education but work in institutions such as these which are not under its control. These centres are for children and young people up to the age of 20 who have learning difficulties and, often, some kind of physical difficulty or medical condition which requires some medical intervention. Pupils follow a curriculum in basic education, life skills and preparation for employment of some kind. Great importance is placed on helping young people to be as independent as possible (Armstrong, 1995). When they leave, some will find ordinary employment and others go on to a protected workshop setting if a place is available.

The process of selection in special education

Decisions concerning the placement of a child in a particular setting are made by District Commissions which were established after the 1975 law of orientation. However, schools are free to admit children with difficulties without the involvement of a commission if they wish to do so. On each commission there are representatives from the Ministry for Education and the Ministry for Health and Social Affairs. There is a commission for children of pre-school and elementary school age and a different one for those of secondary age. These commissions are responsible for drawing up an 'evaluation', which is a document describing the child's difficulties and recommending a particular course of action. This may be to draw up arrangements for a child to be integrated into an ordinary school if they are currently in a special school or institution, or it may recommend removal from an ordinary school to a different setting which could include leaving the education system altogether. Parents are not legally obliged to agree to the recommendations made by the commission.

Integration

Although there appears to be general agreement that most young people with disabilities or difficulties in learning should be included in ordinary schools, there are a great many difficulties to overcome before this is universally accepted in practice. In addition there is little common agreement about what 'inclusion' or 'integration' might mean. The debate about integration has revealed a wide range of differences in interpretation. Are children 'integrated' if they spend all their time in a separate class or unit attached to an ordinary school? Does it make sense to talk of a child being 'integrated' when they attend a school two or three times a week and spend the rest of their time in a day hospital? And can we really talk about 'integration' without including the content and delivery of the curriculum as a major factor in deciding who will be included and and who will be excluded in a common, shared educational system?

Further difficulties arise over the question of statistics. Figures provided by the Ministry for Health and Social Affairs do not make explicit what common criteria were used in gathering statistics on integration and how this term was understood by heads of schools who provided the information (Lantier *et al.*, 1994). It is clear, however, that there are a number of successful initiatives in different parts of France in which children with a range of difficulties and disabilities are being integrated in different ordinary schools. The form and character of these experiences vary according to the ethos of the school and the perceptions of those working with the child, as well reflecting the difficulties the child experiences. In general, these initiatives are taking place at the primary level.

The figures currently available are not recent and cannot fully reflect changes introduced by the 1989 Jospin law and subsequent directives. Some of these have introduced very radical changes which will affect the education of all children, especially in the primary sector (Corbett and Moon, 1995).

In 1990, 16,385 children were integrated at primary level and 8,274 at secondary level. If the figures are broken down, it becomes apparent that some groups of pupils are less likely to attend an ordinary school at secondary level than others. For pupils with a sensory impairment there was a slight reduction of those remaining in the ordinary system at the secondary stage, but for those with learning difficulties the reduction was very large. While 5,987 attended an ordinary school at the primary level, at the secondary stage there were only 620.

The number of pupils with disabilities and learning difficulties who were 'integrated' in 1990 represented 0.23 per cent of the total primary aged population and 0.13 per cent of pupils of secondary age. There was an apparent decrease in the numbers of children integrated, from 28,620 in 1985 to 24,659 in 1990 (Lantier *et al.*, op cit.). More recent figures may show a very different picture. Table 2.2 shows the numbers and percentage of children and young people in special educational provision by categorization in 1989/90.

Table 2.2 Pupils in special educational provision by disability, 1989/90

	Ministry of Education		*Ministry of Social Security*								
			Medical Establishment		*Medical/ Educational Establishment*		*Social/ Educational Establishment*		*Total Ministry Social Security*		*Total of all Establishments*
	No	%	No	%	No	No	%	No	%	No	%
Blind	225	0.1	38	0.2	967	0.9	-	-	1005	0.7	1230
Partially-sighted	1077	0.6	91	0.4	1509	1.4	-	-	1600	1.2	2677
Deaf and partially-hearing	1425	0.7	506	2.4	6961	6.5	45	0.4	7512	5.4	8937
Motor deficiency	2223	1.2	2943	13.7	5649	5.3	35	0.3	8525	6.2	10748
Physical handicap	888	0.5	8355	40.4	40.4	689	0.6	15	0.1	9059	9947
Multiple handicap	12	—	1030	5.0	7445	7.0	43	0.4	8518	6.2	8518
Severe mental retardation	18	—	199	1.0	12507	11.7	18	0.2	12724	9.2	12742
Moderate mental retardation	12251	6.4	197	1.0	28390	26.6	85	0.8	28672	20.8	40923
Slight mental retardation	92461	48.5	234	1.1	13834	13.0	138	1.3	14206	10.3	106667
Emotional problems	4215	2.2	2102	10.2	15121	14.2	1065	10.0	18288	13.2	22503
Psychiatric problems	818	0.4	3778	18.2	6817	6.4	92	0.9	10687	7.7	11505
Social problems	72398	37.9	1335	6.4	6890	6.4	9063	85.6	17288	12.5	89686
Non-handicap	2859	1.5	—	—	—	—	—	—	—	—	2859
Total admitted	190870	100.0	20708	100.0	106777	100.0	10599	100.0	138084	100.0	328954
Total educated	190870	100.0	8313	—	72694	—	5619	—	86626	—	277496

Discussion

The outline presented in this chapter is not exhaustive, but is intended to give some idea of the complexity of provision for children and young people with disabilities or difficulties in learning in France. It also attempts to show some of the points at which the education system and the social and medical provision meet and those where they are quite separate. The separate development of education and the structures and practices relating to health, disability and deviance which have grown up over the past 200 years poses one of the main challenges to a fully inclusive system of education for all.

A further, related issue is the way in which children and young people are assessed and categorized and allocated to different settings or along different routes on the basis of these categories. Categorization has its roots deeply entrenched within the complex apparatus.

The question of those institutional practices which stand in the path of an inclusive educational system and the language which is used as an integral part of those practices is one which all societies need to examine. In some countries, such as the United Kingdom, one set of labels has been got rid of only to be replaced by another set and the insidious blanket term 'special educational needs'. While some groups of children can now get past the door of ordinary schools, other groups with new labels such as 'emotional and behavioural disorders' are denied access. The inclusion of pupils described as having severe learning difficulties is not seriously on the agenda. There are real upheavals taking place in some aspects of education in France. In primary schools, greater emphasis is being placed on meeting the individual needs of all children so that their individual styles and rhythms of learning are taken into account (Corbett and Moon, op.cit.). There are plans to introduce changes to the curriculum to allow for greater flexibility. It is too soon to assess what changes these will bring about in relation to children with disabilities and difficulties in learning.

References

Armstrong, F.J.(1995) '*Appellation Controllée*: Mixing and sorting in the French education system', in Potts, P., Armstrong, F.J., and Masterton, M. *Equality and Diversity in Education 2: National and International Contexts*, London, Routledge.

Ballarin, J-L. (1994) *Enfants difficiles, structures specialisée*, France, Nathan pédagogie.

Bouissou, R. (1967) *Histoire de la médecine* (Encyclopédie Larousse de poche), Paris, Larousse

Corbett, A. and Moon, R.E. (1995) *Change and Continuity in French Schooling: the Mitterand Years 1981–1995*, London, Routledge.

Lantier N., Verillon, J-P., Aublé, B., Belmont, B. and Waysand, E. (1994) *Enfants Handicapés A L'-Ecole: Des instituteurs parlent de leurs pratiques*, Paris, L'Harmattan

Further Reading

Broadfoot, P. and Osborn, M. (1991) 'French Lessons: comparative perspectives on what it means to be a teacher', *Comparative Education: Lessons of cross-national comparisons in education*, 1.

Daunt, P. (1991) *Meeting Disability: A European Response*, London, Cassell.

Foucault, M. (1989) *Madness and Civilization, A History of Insanity in the Age of Reason*, London, Tavistock/Routledge.

Galton, M. and Blyth, A. (1989) *Handbook of Primary Education in Europe*, London, David Fulton

Labregére, A. (1990) *L'Insertion de Personnes Handicapées*, Paris, La Documentation Francaise.

Lafay, H. (1990) *L'Intégration Scolaire des Enfants et Adolescents Handicapées*, Paris, La Documentation Francaise.

O'Hanlon, C. (1993) *Special Education: Integration in Europe*, London, David Fulton

Sharpe, K. (1992) 'Educational homogeneity in French primary education: a double case study,' *British Journal of Sociology of Education*, 13, 3.

CHAPTER 3

A View of Integration in Germany

Dirk Randoll

Preliminary remarks

Writing a critical contribution on the development and state of integrating or including children with handicaps into schools appears particularly fruitful within the context of the international comparison attempted in this book, especially if one wants to learn from mistakes and problems and to contribute to the improvement of educational practices. However, such a critical examination is necessarily limited in a one-sided manner to critical comments and unsolved questions requiring answers. Thus, if the following presents criticisms, this should not be seen as diminishing the commitment and work of the many who have contributed to implementing the ideas of inclusive education successfully. Many committed parents, educators, teachers, scientists and politicians have helped to successfully implement inclusive practices in the FRG within a short span of time and to setting very many positive and promising developments in motion.

The development of school integration in the FRG

In the Federal Republic of Germany, the discussion of integrating or including children with handicaps into schools began in the early 1970s after the first inclusive day nurseries and kindergartens had been established as a result of parent initiatives and after the children with handicaps educated there reached school-going age. In particular, the parents of children who had attended integrated kindergartens turned to the educational authorities demanding that children with and without handicaps, who had been together in their pre-school education, should *not* be separated – as traditionally done – into mainstream and special education schools, but should continue to be taught in inclusive and integrated classes. Despite the support of many proponents of the inclusive idea (particularly charitable organizations, educators, teachers, scientists, unions) and despite the recommendations of the Conference of the Ministers of Education and Cultural Affairs (*Kultus Minister Konferenz*) it was only possible to establish the first integrated classes in primary schools after about ten years of intensive debates and legal proceedings. Initially these were predominantly pilot schemes concluded after accompanied evaluation. Up to that point, on account of the school laws, nothing could be changed in the usual educational practice of educating children with handicaps in special schools. However, by establishing the first inclusive classes, the prerequisites for the joint education of children with and without handicaps were created.

The Federal Republic of Germany is a federation, now comprising 16 federal states. As the responsibility for school laws, school organization and financing rests with the individual states, the development of inclusive education as well as its organization diverged considerably both in timing and content. To date, inclusive practice predominate in states governed by the Social Democratic Party, with very divergent approaches, selection procedures and practices. Some federal states continue with the traditional practice of classifying children's handicaps according to the type of disorder and teaching them in corresponding special schools. A few federal states (e.g. Berlin, Hamburg), have refrained from using the term 'handicapped'; rather, the language relates to children requiring special educational support or of children with special needs; the practice of classifying children according to their disabilty is no longer applied. Instead – without exception – the inclusion and integration of all children with handicaps is the aim. In yet other federal states, several types of disabilities are still being discriminated against in the inclusive schooling process (this particularly concerns mentally retarded children, children with behavioural disorders or with multiple handicaps) and there continues to be a differentiation between types and degrees of handicap.

The different developments in implementing inclusive education thus result in the unequal treatment of children with handicaps and children with specific types of disorders in the Federal Republic of Germany. Parents, whose child with a disability is, for example, educated in Bavaria, have little opportunity of having their child included in a mainstream school, because in Bavaria the main focus of policies concerning chlidren with handicaps is the prevention of handicapping conditions and the development of special educational needs. In contrast, parents living in the federal state of Saarland or Hesse by law are free to decide at which school their child with a disability is to be taught: a primary school near their place of residence or the appropriate special school. The problem of unequal chances and opportunities in the education of children with special needs across the whole of the Federal Republic is thus predominantly the result of the existing structure of the educational system in the FRG and consequently difficult to change. It would thus be desirable to create uniform legal regulations in all federal states that guarantee that parents of children with handicaps are free to choose the school their child should attend. Similarly, more intensive efforts regarding those children with handicaps whose parents have little interest in becoming actively involved on account of their social status would be desirable.

In the following sections, several specific problems of school integration will be discussed, beginning with the fundamental debate on its theoretical foundation and ranging to such matters as concrete practical educational problems.

The theoretical foundations of inclusive education

Fundamentally – largely implicitly – in demanding the inclusion of children with handicaps into mainstream education, it is always assumed that integration is good and segregation, i.e., special education, is bad. On closer examination this polarization, which is repeatedly voiced as an argument in discussions on the reasons for the respective school type by proponents and opponents of inclusive education, appears to be too undifferentiated. Seen in the historical perspective of the special education of children with handicaps, the main motive for separating children with handicaps from the mainstream schools was to create a protected space in which they could freely develop their personalities. In theory the reference group phenomenon on which this approach is based has been empirically confirmed in various contexts and its content can be summarized as implying that children with handicaps feel considerably more integrated emotionally and socially among their equals, than in reference groups of children without handicaps – at least for the time spent at school.

In contrast, the arguments voiced by adherents of the stigmatization theory maintain that because of the separation, a high social distance develops between children with handicaps and children without handicaps, as a result of which stigmatization processes develop or are encouraged and therefore prejudice towards children with disabilities in society is maintained.

Both theories have a justified existence and range of validity, and both can be called upon to empirically support either one or the other form of schooling i.e., either inclusive or special education. On account of this, inclusive education can neither be empirically verified or falsified – as is often incorrectly assumed (Bleidick, 1988). It is and remains a normative decision, even if critical empirical comparative studies of the effects of inclusion have indicated more disadvantages than advantages with respect to the social and emotional integration of pupils with handicaps in integrated classes in the past. Consequently, both school forms have a justified existence and aim at comparable goals using different methods: the integration of people with handicaps into society. Thus, at present, it appears inappropriate to propagate an all-or-nothing demand (either special or inclusive schools). Rather, one should respect the various forms of schooling for children with handicaps and acknowledge their respective methods and goals.

Diagnostics

In many of the federal states which practise inclusive education, the traditional approach of examining and classifying children to determine their need for special education has been retained, i.e., special supportive committees that decide on the type and degree of handicap as well as on the possibilities of pedagogical interventions. However, it does not make sense to promote integration while at the same time continuing to classify children with respect to types of handicap and to record this fact, if this is not done to promote the expert's diagnostic evaluation regarding supportive measures.

How problematic such a labelling or classification process and the categories on which this is based can be, can be exemplified very impressively in the Federal Republic of Germany with regard to the diagnosis of learning disabilities. Analyses of the clinical picture of learning disabilities have shown that the category is not an attribute of the person in the strict sense, but rather depends to a great degree on circumstances outside the individual (e.g., conditions of the school system or normative expectations) and inside the schools (e.g., the possibilities of providing individual supportive measures at the primary school, the entire learning-teaching process). Learning disability is thus primarily an administrative term that only seems to be necessary within the framework of the traditional school system to denote a group of pupils that have to attend a school for children with learning disabilities. Its diagnostic dimensions, 'length', 'degree' and 'extent', appear outdated within the frame of inclusive educational practice and no longer seem practical, because in inclusion completely different goals should be aimed at, goals that do not concern assessing school performance and qualifications but rather with the focus on the social dimensions of the pupil's development. For this reason there is an over-representation of children from foreign families and from socially underprivileged classes in the group of pupils classified as having learning disabilities, and is why learning disabilities are found to an increased extent in areas where special education schools are available.

Teachers

In the various states of the Federal Republic of Germany very different organizational forms of inclusive educational practice can be shown to exist. Even within a single state there are up to six different forms of inclusive practice (e.g., Saarland). Decisive differences exist concerning, for example, the number and composition of children with handicaps to be taught in an integrated class, the supportive aid given to children with handicaps, the teachers collaborating in the class, etc. The results of various scientific evaluations of different models of inclusive education have in the past revealed more advantages than disadvantages of inclusive practices (for an evaluative overview, see Borchert and Schuck, 1992). This can primarily be attributed to the fact that the chosen experimental designs could only lead to the results expected from the outset. Their value and usefulness in evaluating inclusive practice is thus questionable. Critical, comparative studies on the effects of inclusive schooling versus special schooling have rarely been conducted. If, for example, one asks teachers involved in integration contexts about their experiences with this new educational practice, then one obtains findings that differ from the results reported in the many pilot schemes.

In empirical studies conducted by Randoll (1991, 1992) on the effects of integrating children with learning disabilities into mainstream schools, the interviews conducted with teachers revealed some different factors. It should be noted that the teachers involved were able to decide freely whether they wished to teach an integrative class – a practice that is common in most of the federal states; a practice that should definitely be seen in a positive light. The commitment, the interest and the open-mindedness with which the interviewed teachers were prepared to test and experience this new way of teaching is worthy of admiration. However, as their comments showed, the teachers realized fairly soon that they had not been sufficiently prepared for the new tasks, responsibilities and problems confronting them in inclusive teaching. Primary school teachers, who had not learned about methods in special education during the course of their training, nor differential or open forms of teaching, reported that they often felt the task of teaching the class was too over-taxing, working with children with handicaps alongside 'normal' pupils whose behaviour became increasingly 'pathological'. They were given little opportunity to prepare themselves for the altered educational practice. Rather, they were mainly left to cope for themselves and experienced a high degree of additional work load (even though their hours of teaching were less than usual). This is one of the reasons why very many of the primary school teachers said that in future they would no longer want to teach an integrated class.

In contrast, special education teachers, who were used to teaching their own special education class, are often being employed as peripatetic teachers, travelling from school to school and class to class, so as to be able to provide children with handicaps with a few hours of supportive teaching per week. These teachers reported that they missed the prolonged association with one class and the teaching staff of one school. Many of them think that the idea of integration is good; however, its practical implementation, in this way, was considered highly unsatisfactory. The collaboration and cooperation between primary and special education teachers appears particularly problematic, if both do not exhibit a high measure of tolerance and open-mindedness. On the one hand, special education teachers enjoy a higher occupational status, that manifests itself in a salary which, compared to primary school teachers, is considerably higher (and some of the special education teachers fear they will lose these privileges within the context of the further development of inclusive schooling). On the other hand, most special education teachers are better prepared and qualified to deal with difficult pupils, which could, among other things, lead to envy and personal depreciation on the part of primary school teachers and considerably impair collaboration. Furthermore, many teachers criticized the fact that the parents of children without handicaps in inclusive classes and schools did not support the work of the teachers sufficiently, which was also recognizable in the fact that contact between children with handicaps and others outside of school was limited.

The improvement of pre- and in-service training of teachers who work in integrated classes has been demanded for quite a while by different parties. The attendance at special education seminars for teachers in mainstream schools, the improvement of didactic skills for children with handicaps and the planning of individual and differentiated teaching, as well as training in team-teaching, are but a few examples of what needs to be done in this respect.

Transition from primary school to the secondary school level

With the completion of primary schooling, the last point in time is reached to answer the question, which school can continue the work of inclusion in mainstream: short-course secondary school, intermediate school or gymnasium? In the past it could frequently be observed that after the completion of primary school, the inclusion of children with handicaps into mainstream education also came to an end. These children were transferred to a fifth class in a special school after completing the fourth class in a primary school, a state of affairs that is certainly detrimental to the idea of integration.

In the FRG, pupils are assigned to various school types in the secondary sector according to their school performance. This means that at this level the performance aspect has an increased significance, aimed at achieving a fairly homogeneous learning group with respect to academic achievement. In contrast to most other types of secondary schools, the inclusive comprehensive schools that have been established in some federal states work according to the principle of goal-differentiated learning in groups that are heterogeneous with respect to performance. For this reason this is the type of school most often chosen to continue inclusive education – depending of course on the pupil's specific handicap. However, in some federal states the number of comprehensive schools is very limited, so that it is difficult to find adequate mainstream secondary schools for specific groups of children with specific handicaps (e.g., mentally retarded children or those with learning disabilities). Apart from this, it has become known that many comprehensive schools have been opposed to accepting handicapped children as long as the prerequisites concerning space, practical matters and personnel have not been fulfilled. As yet we in the FRG have had little experience with the inclusion of pupils with disabilities into the secondary sector because the inclusive practice in the primary sector has only in the last years developed to such an extent that children are now reaching the age of transfer to a secondary school. In most federal states, several pilot schemes are at present being tested under scientific supervision; these also cover the inclusion of pupils with handicaps into vocational schools.

Grades

The assessment of the school performance of children with different learning predispositions and opportunities is extremely difficult with regard to the criteria used. Some federal states have refrained from the practice of graded reports; instead, individual, written reports evaluating academic achievement are compiled. After primary school, however, the traditional assessment procedures (graded reports) are once again applied. In most cases pupils then receive a report containing the remark that they have, for example, been taught according to the curriculum of a special school for pupils with learning disabilities. It could be shown that the aim of refraining from giving grades, namely assessing the school performance of handicapped children with learning disabilities according to intra-individual standards, i.e., their own learning progress, and not, as usual, according to inter-individual standards, i.e., in comparison to others, particularly to normative measures, has not been attained (e.g., Haeberlin *et al.*, 1991; Randoll, 1991, 1992). Furthermore, pupils with learning disabilities taught in inclusive classes developed a lower self-concept of their school performance abilities than those attending a special school, even though their school performances were better.

As long as schools focus on academic achievement as a primary substantive aim, the practice of inclusion has little chance of being realized in this respect. In the primary sector one might still be able to cope with this problem. However, after transition into the secondary sector when pupils are differentiated according to the quality of their performance and transferred to the respective types of school, it will become increasingly evident.

Financing

In connection with realizing the inclusion of pupils with handicaps into mainstream schools, many federal states are propagating the so-called 'zero option', or cost neutrality. This means that the integration should not be more expensive than the special education of pupils with handicaps. Because of the lack of financial resources in the educational sector, increasingly, educational integration is soon confronted with restrictions to its realization. For example, the school law of Hesse, dated June 17 1992 (*GVBL*, p. 233 ff.) that came into force in the school year 1993/94, states that the school authority has to reject parents application for integration 'if at the chosen general school the special and personnel requirements necessary for the special educational measures are not given or the necessary technical aids or special teaching and learning resources are not available' (§ 54, paragraph 2 (4)).

This can be taken to mean nothing else but that realizing school integration is decisively dependent on the available financial and human resources. Consequently, this led to the fact that for the school year 1991/92 in the federal state of Hesse only 396 of the 1,623 applications by parents for mainstream education of their handicapped children were acceded to, because the necessary resources were not available. It also has to be expected that in rural areas the financial resources for inclusive education will not be sufficient. The motto of many educational politicians is thus: 'Integration? yes! but with as little expenditure as possible!' Propagating cost-benefit analyses with regard to disadvantaged persons as a basis for the idea of including pupils in mainstream schools in a country as rich as the FRG seems highly unsatisfactory.

Conclusion

The idea of inclusive education is good. However it is, in part, based on ideologies and Utopian concepts that can hardly be carried out in reality. The various pilot schemes show several very positive approaches and have achieved positive results; however, many expectations have not been fulfilled to date. This particularly refers to the social and emotional integration of pupils with handicaps, i.e., their acceptance by other pupils in the class. Socio-demographic studies conducted in integrated classes all indicate that pupils with handicaps (especially mentally retarded children or those with learning disabilities or behavioural disorders) very often belong to the marginal group of the class. The self-assessments of these pupils confirm this. These indicate clearly the superiority of some form of special education (reference-group effect). The same tendencies are also visible with respect to achievement motivation in integration which can be regarded as essential for enjoying learning and school in general and is an important personality variable. As yet, not enough research has been conducted on whether and what changes in the attitudes of pupils towards peers with handicaps occur as a result of inclusive education, i.e., whether it reduces prejudice and whether stigmatization is relativized. Even though initial studies seem to indicate positive effects, it remains to be seen whether this can be confirmed in other studies using different designs. This should definitely not be seen as a plea for more empiricism at schools, nor a plea for making a good idea dependent on empirical findings. Rather, one should test the idea of inclusion using the integrated practice itself so as to continue to improve it and to relativize exaggerated expectations.

References

Bleidick, U. *Betriffi Integration. Behinderte Kinder in Allgemeinen Schulen*, Berlin.

Borchert, J. and Schuck, K.D. (1992), *Integration: Ja! Aber wie?*, Ergebnisse aus Modellversuchen zur Forderung behinderter Kinder und Jugendlicher, Hamburg.

Haeberlin, U. *et al.*, (1991), *Die Integration von Lembehinderten*, Versuche, Theorien, Forschungen, Entäuschungen, Hoffnungen, Bern, Stuttgart.

Randoll, D. (1991), *Lernbehinderte in der Schule. Integration oder Segration?*, Studien und Dokumentationen zur verleichenden Bildungsforschung Band 51. Kbln, Wein.

Randoll, D. (1991), *Die schulische Integration Lernbehinderter und ihre Wirksamkeit Ergebnisse eiser Langsschnittstudie*, Viereljahreszeitschrift für Heilpü-dagogik und ihre Nachbargebeite, 61, 3, 376–91.

CHAPTER 4

Inclusive Education: The Greek Experience

V. Lampropoulou, and S. Padeliadou

Introduction

Provision of social services for people with disabilities in Greece dates back to the first decade of this century and has laid the foundation for the development of the field of special education. However, extended educational services are recent and inclusive education has only been the latest outcome of the above process, bearing old, inherited features.

The first steps in providing special services in Greece were made by charity organizations or the church. Their orientation was mostly towards caring for peoples' everyday needs, providing shelter and food, and having usually an institutionalized structure. People with special needs were perceived as totally dependent, inspiring feelings of pity, or as invalids, whose educational training was not a primary consideration.

Efforts in the area of providing special educational services were dominated by private organizations, with the public sector being involved minimally until the 1970s and were strongly influenced by the international experience. However, while in other Western countries the development of special education has been the outcome of the active participation of people with special needs themselves, and of parents and professionals, in Greece international influence and imitation has been the major contributing factor towards this development. All major changes have occurred through administrative actions rather than as an outcome of the pressure of the people involved.

The development of special education has a long history of segregated growth, in terms of legislation, of organizational management and of content/curriculum development. From 1972, when the first legislation about special education was introduced, up to 1985, all legislative actions have existed outside the mainstream educational law (Stasinos, 1991). Law 1143/85 was the first comprehensive law pertaining to special education, which came along to legislate for the existing segregation. Special education structures developed outside the Ministry of Education, while management, organizational structures and supervision were controlled by other Ministries, mainly the Ministry of Health and Welfare. This long history of segregation at all levels has made inclusive education difficult and not a natural evolution based on the national school experience and the needs of internal educational forces.

Development in three phases

The picture of inclusive special education today reflects both the intentions and the reality. The intentions as expressed and described in the booklet of information published in 1991 by the Directory of Special Education are clearly stated:

> The school integration of children with special needs is the major goal of our educational policy (p.18). ...the modern educational and social trends, demands and prospects dictate that the treatment of the child with special educational needs be done discretely, systematically, with understanding and responsibility within the regular school. In a school for all... (p.20).

The same intentions are also expressed in several statements by the authorities in each subsequent year. However, Law 1566/85, the recent law about special education, is less clear about inclusive education and, most significantly, much less specific on how inclusive education ought to be implemented and managed. According to this law the goals of special education are:

> (a) the total and effective development and use of their (students') abilities and capabilities, and (b) their (students') acquisition of the necessary skills leading to an adequate vocational and social integration.

It is evident that the law considers integration the ultimate goal of special education, but it leaves completely open the issue of how and when this integration should begin or how it should be applied within the educational system. It does not provide for alternative inclusive education models. The above lack of specificity allows for development towards any possible direction and any possible mistake, too.

In regard to the practice of inclusive education, there is no systematic recording of all the inclusive education projects or initiatives in the Greek schools thereby making the drawing of conclusions especially difficult. This lack of systematic, valid and reliable data regarding inclusive education in Greece sets limits to any comprehensive evaluation study, since the only data available come from sporadic articles or Reports to the Ministry of Education and the Reports of the European Community for the Helios I Project.

After examining available evidence on the forces and the main characteristics of recorded inclusive special education in Greece, one can detect three distinct chronological phases.

1. 1906–1984: The hidden or invisible inclusion

The first recorded cases of inclusive education in Greece date back to 1981, when students with borderline and mild mental retardation were included at the elementary and secondary level for some school subjects (Spetsiotis, 1991). Those cases were exceptional and were the outcome of personal initiatives of pioneer educators. They preceded any legal or state initiative and represented individual efforts since, during the same period, the main state efforts were oriented towards establishing special schools as separate school structures. Unfortunately, very little has been recorded about the system and the results of those efforts, thus offering minimal information regarding the contributing factors to successful inclusive education. Nevertheless, what we have available on those efforts indicates that, for certain categories of special needs, inclusive education comes easily as a choice even when state policy does not promote it, just because it seems 'the right thing to be done for the kids'.

2. 1984–1989: The special class/resource room expansion

During the second phase, the establishment of many resource rooms seemed to be the major state policy. From 1984 to 1992, the number of special education resource rooms grew from seven to 520. At the same time, the number of special schools grew from 139 to 186 (see Table 4.1).

The increase in the number of special classes since their establishment in 1983–84 reflects the trend of the Greek educational system towards this form of inclusive education. Most of those classes have served children with learning disabilities, mild mental retardation and

Table 4.1 Data on the development of special education programmes in Greece from 1983 to 1992

Academic year	*Special schools*	*Resource rooms*
1983–84	139	7
1984–85	142	25
1985–86	152	105
1986–87	150	141
1987–88	160	221
1988–89	164	285
1989–90	170	368
1990–91	183	460
1991–92	186	520

(*Source*: Booklet of Information on Special Education, 1991)

behavioural problems while several of them have addressed the educational needs of students coming from socially deprived groups. The choice of special education classes as a form of inclusive education has been an attempt on the part of the Greek educational system to combine: (a) the need for serving students with special needs and (b) the need to keep abreast of developments occurring in other developed nations. Therefore, approximately 56.3 per cent of the students with special needs are currently being served in special classes while the rest are served in special schools (EEC, 1992). However, special classes function without specialist personnel, without specially selected material, and often without special organizational arrangements. Nevertheless, placing children with special needs in that environment has seemed to increase pressures for more integration.

Most students with special needs are supposed to spend at least 80 per cent of their school time in their regular education classroom and only go to the resource room for special help, mostly for reading and maths (Polychronopoulou, 1991). However, in actual fact, in many cases students stay full-time in the resource room/special class, either because there is no special school available in the area, or because of their parents' wish (Apostolidis, 1992). Examining data from 1987–88, it seems that only 15 per cent of the children singled out to join a resource room service were re-integrated into their old regular class the following year (Polychronopoulou, 1991). This underscores the role of the resource rooms as a continuous supportive feature in the educational process and not merely as a means of receiving remedial help to overcome specific learning problems. Regarding the qualifications of the teachers working in the resource rooms, few are special education teachers. The majority only have experience in working in regular education, some have attended seminars on special education and very few have had postgraduate training in special education (Apostolidis, 1992; Lampropoulou, 1994).

3. 1989–1993: The European influence

During the third phase, within the framework of the European programme, HELIOS 1, integration efforts have flourished and have also gained the support of the state. Most of those efforts have been restricted to the area in or around the city of Athens, with some additional projects in the rest of Greece. During this period, the term 'inclusive education' has taken various formats and modes of expression. The resource room format continues to be implemented but there is a trend towards applying more comprehensive forms of integration, especially full-time integration. The categories of students with special needs more often involved in inclusive education projects have been the visually impaired, the hearing impaired, the learning disabled and the mentally retarded.

For the group of students with learning disabilities the format followed has been the resource room, judged, with few exceptions, as adequate inclusion for them (Ministry of Education, 1988), wherein full-time inclusion was also attempted. For the group of blind students, the model chosen for implementation has been one of full-time inclusion in a regular class, where two-teacher teams teach (Liodakis, 1991). One of the teachers is specialized in teaching the blind. The students follow the same curriculum as the rest of their classmates, in addition to their training in mobility, Braille, etc. after school in the special school for the blind. The results, as evaluated by the team of teachers who carried out the project, were positive. The major point stressed, though, was that even with two teachers the usual number of 30 to 35 students in an inclusive class with four to five blind students is too high, and needs to be reduced if inclusion is to be effective. For the group of the hearing impaired, both full-time and part-time inclusion into a regular class has been tried (Agaliotis, 1992). In both cases a special educator helped the children in their class and the children were equally well adjusted. However, the lack of qualified teachers, which is almost always the case, makes inclusion a precarious process at the best of times (Birtsas, 1989; Pliakopanos, 1990). For the group with mental retardation, the model most often applied has been that of integrating students for special subjects in the regular/mainstream class (Hatzopoulos and Anagnostou, 1991). The students are carefully selected and they receive no help in the regular class. The special subjects are drama, art, mythology and history, or subjects selected according to the needs of the individual student (Christakis, 1991). In some cases full-time inclusion for children with almost borderline intelligence or mild retardation has also been tried (Stamatis, 1991). In all cases reported, the students with retardation have been well accepted by the rest of the students and are well adjusted. However, as underlined by those reporting on the projects, the major difficulty with this population is to find regular education teachers who will accept mentally retarded students in their classes.

Inclusive education in Greece has also made significant inroads at the pre-school stages. A small number of children with special needs still receive education in segregated pre-school settings, while a number of full-time inclusive placements have been attempted either within the Helios Programme or, in very few isolated cases, by the teachers' own initiative. It appears that inclusive education at the pre-school level is manageable and more acceptable than at the higher educational levels. The children learn to play and live together, the educators learn to accept the children with special needs. Also the pre-school can make adjustments to provide assistance to the educators (Simeonidou, 1986).

It would appear that the history of inclusive education in Greece, albeit brief, has come full circle, imparting a number of valuable lessons. We know that students can be included in the mainstream without any guarantee that this inclusion brings the best results. We know that special education classes (resource rooms) can accommodate some of the students with special needs but we do not know what trained teachers could do in the same environment. Nevertheless, the major question for any choice remains: how can we serve students with special needs the best way in mainstream education without depriving them or the students in the mainstream of any necessary educational service?

In a nutshell, it will have become clear that special education in Greece is fraught with major problems. This is strongly highlighted by the lack of special curriculum, special materials and, most significantly, specially trained teachers and the support of other needed professionals, such as speech therapists and psychologists. These weaknesses have all been amply documented in the literature as well as in the national reports of the Directory of Special Education.

Major considerations

The idea of inclusive education for students with special needs is morally correct and philosophically progressive. However, the implementation of inclusive education is constrained by the many limitations imposed by prevailing realities. Sharing the ideas of equal rights to education, equal access to everyday activities and facilities and the right to social inclusion are definitely important prerequisites for any further development. But it should be borne in mind that such prerequisites are not in themselves sufficient to guarantee successful implementation, unless a variety of factors are controlled, guided and planned effectively. It is not simply the idea of equal rights for students with special needs but the specific interpretation of 'what equal means', that creates the disagreements and conflicts among educators.

Our experience in Greece has revealed to us that the factors influencing successful inclusive education should rely not only on special education – as the education to be included – but mostly on the structure and developments in regular education – the education to be included into. The attitudes and knowledge of regular education teachers, the curriculum content, the school structure and the characteristics of the students themselves are all interrelated parameters to be considered in implementing any degree or form of inclusive education. It is our belief that effective inclusive education in Greece will have to address especially the factors discussed below, in order to become beneficial to children with special needs.

Regular education teachers

Inclusive education is based on the assumption that teachers in the mainstream of education *wish* to and *can* accommodate students with special needs in their classes. In regard to the first part of this assumption, a recent study conducted by the Aristotelian University of Thessaloniki has shown that teachers (n=140) have a negative attitude towards inclusive education (Padeliadu, 1992). Moreover, college students trained to become teachers (Department of Primary Education in Thessaloniki (n=360) and Department of Primary Education in Florina (n=52)), although less negative than the practicing teachers, do not appear positive towards inclusive education for students with special needs (Padeliadu, 1993).

In regard to the second part of the assumption, that teachers can accommodate the special needs of exceptional students in the regular education class, a number of questions can be raised. The vast majority of regular education teachers (89.3 per cent) do not feel competent to teach students with special needs in their regular education class. Furthermore, one out of five of the same teachers were found to provide absolutely no assistance when confronted with special needs students in their class (Padeliadu, 1992). In addition, regular education teachers who are placed in resource rooms seem to set as their first priority the acquisition of special training (Lambropoulou, 1994; Padeliadu, 1992). Furthermore, future teachers appear to have very little knowledge (20-25 per cent correct responses, depending on the category of special needs) about the instructional implications of each special needs category (Padeliadu, 1993).

This lack of knowledge on the part of both the teachers and the teachers to be, in conjunction with the lack of structures for training specialized teachers, does not allow for much optimism about the successful implementation of inclusive education. Currently, the single school of postgraduate training for special education in Greece, Maraslios school, functioning outside university jurisdiction, provides a two-year training course for a limited number of teachers. This number is not adequate considering the number of special education units in operation today and the prospective needs, if inclusive education is to expand. Furthermore, the courses offered in this programme are general in nature and do not lead to any specialization. Moreover, in all university-level departments of education in Greece, the courses in special education offered are limited and rarely compulsory, indicating that the future teachers will not be adequately equipped for the implementation of an effective inclusive education.

The structure of regular education

Students are enrolled in regular education classes on the basis of age and are exposed to all aspects of the curriculum as a group. Each class usually includes 30–35 students and is taught by one teacher. The instructional approach employed by the teachers in Greece (except for a very few cases) is whole-class instruction, with very little individualization. Lately, an intensive evaluation routine has been established, which forces teachers and students to keep up with certain standards of achievement. The above two conditions create a competitive classroom environment, with little room for differentiation, wherein students need to fit in completely to avoid being excluded. This environment will need to be altered significantly for inclusive education to take place. Inclusive education requires individualization of instruction, small group instruction, alternative grouping and instructional methods, differentiated procedures and flexible evaluation criteria and achievement standards. In comparing the requirements of inclusive education with the current structure and orientation of regular school in Greece, the existing distance between the needs of the regular and special education students is obvious and the need for changes in the mainstream becomes a major consideration.

A thorough and comprehensive evaluation of what inclusive education will mean for mainstream education is needed in order to ensure the best services for all children. Unfortunately, past and current policy-making do not intimate any such comprehensive appraisal, aiming as it does towards implementing inclusive education with no alterations of any type to the mainstream curriculum and educational structures.

Systematic approach

Currently, a significant number of students with special needs are being taught in the mainstream of education, either by choice or by chance. The screening process for special needs students is almost non-existent, while existing assessment teams and centers cannot cover all present needs for systematic diagnosis and placement, despite their immense efforts. Students are often placed in a special education unit, special school or class, only after a superficial assessment is undertaken or by agreement between the school personnel, the parents and the special education teacher (Papatheophilou, 1990). Students with special needs are being identified by their regular education teachers and are placed in special education based on criteria and processes vaguely defined by the law and even more vaguely implemented in everyday practice. For all those children who have been placed, one way or another, in special education units, there is no procedure established for reintegration into the mainstream. In Law 1566/85, there are no specific guidelines or processes for re-examining the cases of students placed in special education and no special criteria for re-entering the mainstream. Moreover, special education units do not apply the Individualized Educational Programme process, failing thus to ensure objective and systematic evaluation of students' progress. Therefore, the degree of inclusive education for each student is not determined by a systematic and scientific approach but is left to the subjective decisions of parents and teachers or to mere coincidence.

Supportive structures

Providing special education for students who need it should not be perceived as a special infrastructure. It should involve special services, materials, methods and approaches addressing the special child's educational needs. The international experience of special education and inclusive education has produced a variety of models alternative to the separate system, such as consultation centers within each school, centers of instructional material and methodology, use of support personnel, team teaching, use of aids in the class, etc. However, national conditions have very little in common with all the above supportive structures. On the one hand, there is a complete lack of support services within the structure of regular schools, leading any mainstream students facing even small problems to special education. On the other hand, special education as it is can not accommodate the special needs of students due to shortcomings in materials, personnel and programmes. In sum, serious limitations characterize the type of special education offered in Greece at the present time and also predetermine the level of success for inclusive education.

Conclusions

After examining the history of the development of special education in Greece, one can identify two main obstacles to implementing quality inclusive education for children with special needs: (a) insufficient planning at all levels on the part of the government, and (b) the lack of participation of the people directly involved (parents, professionals, people with special needs) in the decision-making and planning processes. All major developments in the area of special education, and specifically of inclusive education, have been introduced by the government in an attempt to address the needs of a special population of students and to assuage immediate political expediency, rather than after systematic and long-term planning.

None the less, inclusive special education is a reality at the present time in Greece. This very reality imposes new priorities and alerts to the need for the identification of key issues that have to be resolved. More responsible, data-based planning has to take place. This is not to imply that research data alone could offer a yes or no answer for inclusive education since the issue also has considerable moral relevance. However, research can guide and assist in making decisions as to the best way for inclusive education to be implemented and can function as a shield against political pressures and financial cutbacks (Biklen, 1985). Major questions such as – which types of special needs should be catered for by inclusive education? When should inclusive education start? What kind of training should teachers receive for inclusive education? Should this training precede inclusive education? – are serious, demanding serious answers. Furthermore, attitudes, cost, organization and management issues need to be carefully pondered to pre-empt purely cosmetic measures.

Undoubtedly, developments in the field of inclusive education should be accomplished cautiously, although it would be a grave mistake to stifle it on the grounds that a reliable database is not yet available. Empowering the people directly involved, upgrading and extending the available services for the education of students with special needs, should be the first steps for any well-aimed development. Improvement and expansion of special educational provisions at all educational levels will improve the quality of education for all students, regardless of their abilities or needs.

References

Agaliotis, Y. (1992) *Functional School Integration: Evaluation of a project*, 'Because Difference is a Right', 44–45. 21–27.

Apostolidis, A. (1992) *Special Education in 10th Educational District.* Graduation Thesis, Aristotelian University of Thessaloniki, Thessaloniki.

Biklen, D. (1985) *The Complete School: Integrating special and regular Education*, New York, Columbia University, Teacher's College Press.

Birtsas, C. (1989) *Support Teaching Model*, Presentation at the meeting at the European Conference on School Integration, Helios, Rotterdam 25–27 October.

Christakis, K. (1991) *Report on the Program of School Integration of Students of the Model Special School, MTA In Regular Schools*, Report to the Directory of Special Education, Ministry of Education.

European Economic Community, (1992) *Report of the Commission for the Progress of Integration Policy in the educational systems of the member states (1988–1991)*, Commission of the European Communities, Brussels.

Hatzopoulos, A. and Anagnostou, E. (1991) *HELIOS Project at Perama*, Report to the Directory of Special Education, Ministry of Education.

Lampropoulou, V. (1994) *Problems and Issues in Integration in Southern Greece*, unpublished document.

Liodakis, D. (1991) *Implementing school integration with blind students*, Report to the Directory of Special Education, Ministry of Education.

Ministry of Education–Directory of Special Education (1988) *Proceedings of the*

Seminar on Special Education, Ministry of Education–UNESCO, Instuctional Books Publications, Athens.
Padeliadu, S. (1992) *School Integration of Students with Special Needs: The perspective of regular education teachers*, Presentation at the fourth Panhellenic Conference of Social Paediatrics, Kerkyra.
Padeliadu, S. (1993) *Educating Students with Special Needs: Content and perspectives*, Proceedings of the first Greek educational symposium. Association of Teaching Science of Komotini, Komotini.
Papatheophilou, R. (1990) *The Function of Special Classes within the Regular Education Schools: Conclusions of a study*, Seminar in learning disabilities proceedings, Greek Association of Mental Health and Neuropsychiatry of the Child, Athens.
Pliakopanos, S. (1990) *Helios Project at the School for the Deaf and Hard of Hearing*. Report to the Directory of Special Education, Argirouplis.
Polychronopoulou, S. (1991) *Mainstreaming Systems in Greece*, Presentation at the meeting of the Greek Representatives of Helios 1 Project.
Simeonidou, E. (1986) Argo, *Because Being Different is a Right*, 14–15, 125–9.
Spetsiotis, Y. (1991) *Project of Including Special Needs Children in the Regular Schools*, Report to the Directory of Special Education, Ministry of Education.
Stamatis, S. (1991) *Activities Within the Integration Project Helios*, Report to the Directory of Special Education, Ministry of Education.
Stasinos, D. (1991) *Special Education in Greece. Perspectives, institutions and practice, public and private Initiative (1906-1989)*, Athens, Gutenberg.

CHAPTER 5

Integration in Ireland: Policy and practice

Patricia Lynch

Background information

Compulsory schooling in Ireland extends from 6 to15 years of age. There is no country-wide state-funded pre-school education although there is a pilot scheme in operation as of September 1994. In any case, most 4-year-old children and almost all 5-year-old children are enrolled in primary schools. The vast majority of pupils remain in school until the age of 17 or 18. The proportion of the total population of children in the 6 to 15 year age bracket enrolled in special schools is 1.2 per cent (Ireland, 1990).

Special education – development

Special education services in Ireland began to expand in the late 1950s. At that time, if a child was found to have serious special educational needs (SEN), the special school was the common form of provision except in areas where numbers were too small. In such instances, special classes were established in ordinary schools in central towns. By the 1970s new provision for children with SEN was shifting from special school placement to special class placement in mainstream schools.

Ireland is somewhat unusual within the European Union because it has the lowest population density of any member state. Over 40 per cent of its schools have three teachers or less, so there are mixed age and ability levels in each class grouping. This would seem to be a ready-made opportunity for children with SEN to be fully included in mainstream schooling. It goes without saying that extra support would be essential, either directly to the pupil or indirectly through the class teacher.

Provision for pupils with SEN in Ireland is made in both special and ordinary schools. This country still uses the traditional categories of disability long since abandoned by many other countries to describe and determine provision. While most countries use terms like 'special educational needs' or 'learning difficulties' (sometimes specifying degrees of difficulty by the terms mild, moderate, severe and profound), Ireland is still differentiating between at least 11 different categories of disability/learning difficulty. The term 'handicap' is still used in official documents, in reports, in lectures and in conversations. For purposes of clarification, children identified as functioning below an assessed IQ of 70 are considered to be mentally handicapped, either to a mild (IQ 50–70), moderate (IQ 35–50), severe (IQ 20–35) or profound (IQ 0–20) degree. Depending on their assessed IQ, children with a mental handicap are generally placed in a special school or a special class in an ordinary school. Almost all pupils with sensory and physical disabilities are fully integrated into mainstream education. Those who need extra support would receive it from a visiting teacher or a resource teacher.

While Ireland was one of the first European countries to provide education on a general basis for children with a moderate level of mental handicap, the educational system has yet to include all children with learning difficulties. There are still over 1,000 children who are assessed as functioning within the severe and profound levels of intellectual ability who are in special care units staffed and run by the Department of Health. Since 1986, approximately 200 children in this group have been taught by teachers on the staffs of special schools in pilot projects set up by the Department of Education. It has been recommended in the Special Education Review Committee Report (SERC, 1993) that the education service should be extended 'to all children and young people with severe and profound mental handicap' (p. 131). The wheels have already been set in motion for that to happen, so in the near future all children of school-going age will be taught by fully qualified teachers within the educational system.

Support teachers in mainstream schools

Ireland has no Education Act yet, no legislation which regulates educational provision for pupils with SEN. However, most pupils with learning difficulties are enrolled in mainstream education and are supported by a rapidly expanding support service. There are different types of teachers offering support to pupils with special educational needs in both primary and post-primary schools. In addition to the three types of support described here – remedial, resource and visiting teacher services – support is also provided by teachers in special classes, guidance counsellors and home-school-community liaison teachers.

Remedial teachers

While it has been acknowledged (Department of Education, 1988; INTO, 1994; Lynch and O'Sullivan, 1986) that the term 'remedial' is not an appropriate term to describe the work of Ireland's remedial teachers, the term continues to be used. Perhaps it is being retained so as to distinguish the target population of the remedial teacher from that of resource and visiting teachers. That is obviously not a good enough reason, and one can only hope that by the time Ireland has its first Education Act, all terms relating to pupils with special educational needs will have been carefuly considered and changed as needed.

Remedial teachers have been employed in schools since the early 1960s. They work with pupils whom Warnock (DES, 1978) referred to as the '18 per cent'. The work of remedial teachers in post-primary schools is generally quite varied. While most of them would be supporting the same type of pupils as their primary school counterparts, others are also working with pupils with more serious learning difficulties (usually because there is no resource teacher in the school) and many are involved in other types of teaching as well, e.g., team-teaching and teaching examination classes.

In 1988 the Department of Education published its *Guidelines on Remedial Education* for primary schools. In addition to describing the current work of the remedial service in its varied forms of provision, the publication set out to offer general guidelines on the aims and organization of remedial education and to address questions faced by all schools as they try to create a learning environment that will meet the needs of all pupils, including those who are experiencing difficulties. The guidelines were intentionally not prescriptive so as not to stifle any innovative practices which emerge from time to time in particular schools. This approach was generally appreciated by the more experienced remedial teachers and yet was criticized by some who were hoping for more specific direction and answers.

The report acknowledged the main concerns coming from remedial teachers themselves, e.g., a conviction that prevention is preferable to remediation, that the widely-practised withdrawal method is not necessarily the most effective way of working, and that the focus on skills development should perhaps be shifting to a wider focus encompassing the total needs of the child. Each of these concerns appears to point to the need for the school itself to take on the responsibility for looking after the needs of all its pupils.

Traditionally, pupils with special educational needs were catered for by one of the three types of support teachers assigned to the school, either on a full-time or part-time basis. More recently, however, there seems to be general agreement that a whole-school effort is necessary to ensure equal opportunities for all pupils. Inclusion will never be a reality here unless schools begin working as a team with full staff involvement to take responsibility for and provide an appropriate education for their pupils with learning difficulties. In describing examples of good practice, the guidelines stated that, 'Planning, co-operation, discussion and organisation were essential for success and the Principal as head of the school was an important agent of change' (p.29).

Most remedial teachers in 1988 were withdrawing pupils from their classrooms to offer help with reading, and to a lesser extent with mathematics. These small group sessions would normally last between 30 and 40 minutes and would normally take place within the remedial teacher's room. Through ongoing contact with remedial teachers over the years, there does not seem to have been any significant change in the way in which these teachers work. Almost all of them are still withdrawing children for sessional help and very few have either initiated a shift in role towards acting as a resource to their class teacher colleagues, nor have they often been asked to do so either by Department of Education inspectors or by principal teachers. As new appointments are made, they tend to continue with the established practice of withdrawal.

The latest figures show that 83 per cent of the total primary school population has access to remedial services. This still leaves a regrettable gap in service which the government is committed to close. An additional 100 remedial teachers were appointed in September 1994 in a move towards achieving this end (INTO, 1994). Most of the new appointments have been to small country schools. These remedial teachers are generally shared between two to five or even six schools in rural areas. One can imagine the inherent difficulties of such an arrangement. A discussion of those difficulties and their resultant inadequacies and injustices is another day's work. However, as regards the issue of integration, it would seem that these teachers are ideally placed to develop a different role for themselves, a role which has been talked about for a long time but has only made sporadic appearances in particular schools. Their time with pupils is limited anyway because of the significant amount of time they spend travelling from school to school and because it is impossible to offer direct help on a day-to-day basis as happens in large city schools. So, they are in a position to develop a role in which they could be offering more direct support to the class teachers and less direct teaching to the pupils. In order to establish themselves in such a role and feel confident about this way of working, they would certainly need some direction, encouragement and support from the Department of Education as well as in-service education. The opportunity is there now and should be seized.

Resource teachers

The name 'resource teacher' does not necessarily reflect the type of work most people understand as resource work. Except for some resource teachers at second level whose balance of work reflects their title, all others with that title seem to be working as additional teachers in a school with little or no meaningful contact with school staffs as regards working in a resource capacity.

Resource teachers were first appointed to post-primary schools in the 1980s as part of a pilot scheme in a limited number of schools. They were meant to provide a continuing service to those pupils who had been in special classes in primary schools. When special classes were established in mainstream primary schools, there was no equivalent provision at second level. When pupils reached the age at which they would normally move on to second level, there was no appropriate facility in these schools to accommodate them. They would either remain in the primary special class until the school-leaving age of 15, or they would transfer to a special school. Either option was unacceptable to all concerned, so pressure was put on the Department of Education to provide the proper support in second level schools. Special classes were established in 16 post-primary schools. Over time, the name of the teachers appointed to such a position has changed from 'special class teacher' to 'resource teacher' in most cases. Their title seems to depend on how they actually operate in their schools.

The appointment of resource teachers at primary level is a recent development. They are employed directly by schools and usually work in a number of small schools in a given area. Their work differs from that of a remedial teacher in that they usually work on an individual basis, withdrawing pupils from mainstream classes who have more serious learning difficulties. At the moment, the resource teachers' expressed concerns include lack of time spent with pupils as well as with class teachers, lack of contact amongst themselves, and a feeling that they are working in total isolation without much direction and without back-up support.

The work of resource teachers in second level schools is quite different from that of resource teachers in primary schools, even though all their pupils have a similar degree of learning difficulty. While all are attached to mainstream schools, some are working in self-contained special classes with little or no integration of their pupils, while others are indeed acting in a resource capacity to their subject-teacher colleagues. The pupils in a self-contained special class generally follow a narrower curriculum than pupils who are integrated with some support. Yet there would seem to be no obvious difference between the curricular capabilities of pupils in these different situations. Some are being afforded more opportunities than others, which raises the issue of equity. Some of the main problems related to their work which were identified by resource teachers are: lack of support, isolation, unclear school policy on special educational needs, lack of role definition, lack of specific training, lack of time for planning and for generally acting as a resource teacher, lack of suitable teaching materials, and lack of certification for those unable to take part in state examinations. Resource teachers expressed an urgent need for in-service courses in areas such as curriculum development, developing self-esteem, integration, organizational models and identification procedures, to name just a few (Lynch and MacCurtain, 1994).

Visiting teachers

A visiting teacher service for pupils with sensory impairments attending mainstream schools has been operating for approximately 20 years. Recently, the Department of Education has restructured the visiting teacher service, increasing the number of teachers within the service, broadening the target population to include pupils with any other serious learning difficulties, and confining their work to smaller geographical areas. Newly appointed teachers to this service are expected to have an extra qualification. For most, that would be the Diploma in Special Education acquired on the only one-year, full-time, in-service generic course in special education. All of these teachers were feeling out of their depth to some extent with the broadening of their brief. While the diploma course afforded knowledge and teaching experience across a wide spectrum of learning difficulty, their own teaching experience over the years in specialized situations had made them competent and confident in one particular aspect of special education. Now they were being asked to address the learning needs of pupils who have other types of difficulties which they may have encountered only briefly in their past experience. They felt the induction course provided by the Department of Education, while helpful, was insufficient to equip them for their changed role and are looking forward to more focused short courses in specific areas to develop their expertise.

Support services: concerns

Lack of direction from the Department of Education and lack of appropriate in-service education have limited the roles of all support teachers. Most still work directly with pupils, usually withdrawing them from their classes for individual or small-group help. They are not, for the most part, functioning as a true resource to their class teacher colleagues. Perhaps they feel insecure working in a cooperative/consultative manner because they have not been prepared for such a role. They have always worked in a room with children only, not with colleagues. Most would have had no previous experience working as a member of an inter-disciplinary team in which ideas are shared, joint conclusions drawn and decisions made as a group. Most resource teachers in post-primary schools, as yet, have had no advanced training in teaching children with serious learning difficulties. If they are still unsure of their own knowledge and skills in teaching such children, should they be expected to offer advice, guidance and support to their colleagues?

It has often been acknowledged that a good support system is, in itself, a form of in-service education. Perhaps this is an ideal time, as Ireland is beginning to expand and develop its system of support services, to ensure that the services are given an appropriate level of funding, that in-service education focused on the particular role of support is provided, and that there is a coordination of effort of all those doing the supporting – whether they are called resource teachers, visiting teachers, remedial teachers or another name which has yet to be invented.

Integration

Development

In most countries, integration, in educational terms, refers to the process by which children with and without special educational needs are educated together in the mainstream school system. The type of integration generally ranges from occasional contact to full participation in the ordinary curriculum. Ireland has a reasonably well developed system of special education, much of which has established itself in the last 40 years. Ireland's population is small and, with the exception of the Dublin area, is relatively scattered. Years ago it was felt that provision for many of the small groups requiring special education would best be offered in special schools. Given the population distribution, this meant residential placement for many children who were far removed from the nearest city.

More recently, there has been a change of thinking regarding residential placement. Parents have been in the forefront in this regard, insisting that their children should be able to attend their own local mainstream schools and should be assisted in doing so by the Department of Education.

Policy

Government policy on integration has been expressed on a few occasions in the recent past. In May 1990, during Ireland's presidency of the European Community, the Minister for Education proposed a resolution on the integration of children with special educational needs. This was adopted unanimously by the EC Council of Ministers of Education. Within the next two years the government published its Green Paper on Education (Ireland, 1992) and stated that policy on integration,

> will seek to provide for children with special educational needs in mainstream schools as far as possible and according as it is appropriate for the particular child. This means that it is accepted that there will continue to be children with disabilities for whom enrolment in an ordinary school would not be appropriate (p. 62).

Practice

When pupils are integrated into mainstream classes, this happens as a result of any number of initiatives. An entire staff may be in favour of full integration of pupils with learning difficulties; the principal may have particularly good leadership qualities, as well as being enlightened, and may put in place from the start a well-integrated system of education; a persistent resource teacher may chip away at staff fears and opposition until they begin to accept his/her pupils with learning difficulties into mainstream classes; a school inspector may insist on full integration with support provided as needed; parent pressure may be brought to bear on a school to provide integrated opportunities. These are only a handful of possibilities – there are many more.

There are no guidelines regarding integration so each school can determine its own arrangements. This is not good enough, as a support teacher could find it quite difficult to overcome all the barriers in a particular school despite his/her best efforts. So, who is responsible for integration policies in a school? It seems to be anybody's and nobody's responsibility. There is no specified or consistent process in place, yet integration is happening on a wide scale. The fact that it is taking place does not imply, of course, that adequate resources are provided.

Inclusive education in its purest sense, of which some countries can boast, is seen by some influential groups in this country as unrealistic, impossible or inappropriate. While all would agree that pupils with SEN should have their needs catered for within the educational system, most support the notion of a continuum of provision from total segregation in special schools to full inclusion in mainstream schools with no additional support required. The INTO (1993) supports the principle of integration, 'in situations where it is in the child's best interests and where the necessary resources to support a child with special needs are provided for the school...integration is not the best educational option for *all* children with disabilities' (p.43).

The SERC Report (Ireland, 1993) maintained that, 'It would neither be possible nor desirable to attempt to cater adequately for every single pupil with disability or special educational needs in every single isolated school' (p.24). The committee recommended regional resource centres situated around the country to provide necessary support services to schools in their areas. The identification of designated schools was also suggested as a means of grouping children in these schools who would need a substantial amount of support. The committee later concluded that, 'There will continue to be a need for some forms of special segregated provision for particular pupils, at least for part of their years in school' (p.63).

Inhibiting factors

While flexibility is built in to the primary school curriculum through its aims and objectives, classroom teachers do not seem to know how to provide adequately for individual learning differences nor how to provide a flexible classroom structure and organization that would accommodate all pupils with varying abilities and needs. There is no requirement at present that initial training courses provide modules in SEN, although most lecturers would make an effort to heighten students' awareness of children with learning difficulties in the classroom. Fortunately, there is now a widely recognized need for a compulsory and substantial input on SEN in initial training in both first and second level training courses (INTO, 1993; Ireland, 1993).

As Ireland has a centralized system of education, with the Government Department of Education based in Dublin, there is no intermediate structure in place between the Department of Education and a school, except for the Vocational Education Committees. In a country with a small population and such a wide scattering of schools, this lack of local administrative structure impedes the efforts of all support teachers as each one works in isolation with individual children without the opportunity to consolidate their efforts within a given area to the wider benefit of class teachers and pupils. The SERC Report (1993) urged the establishment of such local educational administrative structures 'without delay throughout the country' (p.57) so that all services to pupils with SEN would be coordinated.

Special schools have yet to become the centres of expertise envisaged in the Warnock Report. There are very few examples in this country of links between special and mainstream schools. In its response to the Government Green Paper on Education, the Irish National Teachers Organisation (INTO, 1993) recommended that 'special schools should act as resource centres for special classes and mainstream schools, and provide expertise, facilities and services to assist in the education of children with disabilities' (pp.44–5).

In countries where two parallel systems of ordinary and special schools exist, and where the percentage of pupils enrolled in special education is much higher than in Ireland, one would expect enormous problems in breaking down the barriers between the two systems. However, The Netherlands, with approximately 4 per cent of their school-going population in special schools, have made a supreme effort to forge links between special and mainstream schools and have succeeded in a number of ways (Den Boer, 1990). Hegarty (1993) also reported on a variety of successful linkages between special and mainstream schools which could serve as sound examples on which to base pilot projects in this country. The SERC Report (1993) wholeheartedly agrees with the benefits of such linkages, yet reports that 'little constructive effort has been made to set up ongoing linkages between the parallel systems of ordinary and special schools in Ireland' (p.64). The review committee goes on to recommend that resources be made available to encourage such links and suggests ideas for types of cooperative work. These recommendations will hopefully be given serious consideration before the publication of the government's White Paper on Education, the precursor of an Education Act.

Large class sizes, insufficient resources, orientation towards academic/exam success in second level schools, inadequate support services, lack of legislation safeguarding the rights of children with SEN to an appropriate education and stipulating the responsibilities of the state and schools, are all factors which inhibit the successful integration of children with learning difficulties. Lack of research is also an inhibiting factor. While examples of good integration practices abound, as do examples of positive initiatives taken by parents, teachers, schools and the Department of Education, none of these can be said to evolve from research evidence into integration in this country.

Facilitating factors

There are several factors in Irish education that would augur well for children with SEN in mainstream schools. Initial training students are drawn from the top quartile of third-level applicants and the quality of teacher training for primary education is quite high in comparison with many other countries. It has often been said that good sound teaching is one of the most influential factors in a child's learning success.

In addition to good teaching, attitudes towards pupils with SEN must be positive. Studies on attitudes carried out in the recent past indicate very positive attitudes on the part of teachers in mainstream primary schools (Bates, 1993; Lawless and Colfer, 1990; O'Connor, 1988). Studies of parents' attitudes have also been positive. These studies include parents of children with serious learning difficulties (Dunne, 1992) as well as parents of children with no learning difficulties (Carpenter, 1994). Attitudes of principals in mainstream schools were also found to be positive (McCormack, 1990), although principals expressed more concern about sufficient resources than anyone else. In any review of successful integration practices, positive attitudes are cited as a crucial factor. In this regard, the most important factor is already in place in Irish schools. Surveys suggest that the Irish primary school provides a positive context for the development and success of inclusive education, provided, of course, that other important factors such as resources accompany the general goodwill and positive attitudes.

There is an increasing awareness among teachers generally about children's needs and rights as well as a greater knowledge about special educational needs. Parents of children with SEN are also increasingly aware of their right to have their children educated with their siblings and neighbours in their local mainstream schools. Parents of children with Down's Syndrome have been to the forefront in recent years in insisting that their children attend mainstream schools. Parental pressure is alive and well. Parent groups have succeeded in forcing the Department of Education to provide support teachers for their children.

Other factors such as the expansion of the psychological service to primary schools, the increase in appointments of support teachers, falling school rolls, the Government's commitment to integration, the flexibility of the primary school curriculum, and a significant increase in professional development courses for teachers, are all contributing to the likelihood of successful school experiences for all children, but particularly for those with learning difficulties.

The way forward

Barriers need to be broken down between the mainstream and special education systems as well as between the Departments of Education, Health and Justice. The old myths about the 'specialness' of special education must be dispelled so that all teachers and support personnel can work together in the common interests of *all* their pupils. Ireland's primary school curriculum (Ireland, 1971) is indeed child-centred and aims to provide each child with 'the kind and variety of opportunities towards stimulation and fulfilment which will enable him (sic) to develop his natural powers at his own rate to his fullest capacity' (p.13). The curriculum handbook goes on to acknowledge that to achieve this aim, the curriculum must be 'sufficiently flexible to meet the needs of children of widely varying natural endowment and cultural background' (p.13). While the policy of providing an appropriate education to children with diverse needs and abilities has been expressed officially for many years and is well known to all teachers, the practice has yet to match the intention.

The system needs to take a lead in actively promoting a whole-school approach to pupils with learning difficulties. A significant expansion of in-service education, preferably school-based, will be essential in the future for all members of staffs in our schools. This is an area in which Ireland lags far behind some of its European partners, although as of September 1994 major steps have been taken by the Department of Education to improve this situation. The establishment of an In-Career Development Unit is a positive development for the whole area of special needs education, because many of the recent demands for professional development relate to this area. The INTO (1993) has outlined the range of provision of in-service education that should be considered by such a unit and also suggested current issues and topics that should be included as main elements of in-service courses. While only one section applied directly to chldren with special educational needs, almost every other section, e.g., professional and staff development, assessment and evaluation, school organization, held implications for pupils with SEN. The future is looking brighter for all children.

It is encouraging to note that the most important factors related to successful integration practices – good teaching, positive attitudes and a flexible curriculum – are firmly in place in Irish schools. The noted inhibiting factors are all system-wide issues that need to be addressed in the forthcoming White Paper on Education and in the Education Act. These issues need to be given the careful consideration they deserve and essential changes must be made to improve the chances of children with learning difficulties to be fully included in mainstream education with the required support.

If the goal of inclusion is to 'create a community in which all children work and learn together and develop mutually supportive repertoires of peer support' (Stainback, *et al.*, 1994, p.486) while at the same time catering for childrenJs individual differences, then Ireland should find it relatively easy to move towards an inclusive system of education once the system offers its full support.

References

Bates, B. (1993) 'Attitudes towards integration: A survey of teachers', *Education Today*, 1 2, 11–12.

Carpenter, B. (1994) 'Shared learning: The developing practice of integration for children with severe learning difficulties', *European Journal of Special Needs Education*, 9 2, 182–89.

Den Boer, K. (1990) 'Special education in the Netherlands', *European Journal of Special Needs Education*, 5, 2, 136–49.

Department of Education and Science (1978) *Special Educational Needs* (The Warnock Report). Londo:; HMSO.

Dunne, S. (1992) 'Special education: A time for change', *Reach*, 7, 1, 3–11.

Hegarty, S. (1993) 'Reviewing the literature on integration', *European Journal of Special Needs Education*, 8, 3, 194–200.

Ireland, Department of Education (1971) *Primary School Curriculum.* Dublin: The Stationery Office.

Ireland, Department of Education (1988) *Guidelines on Remedial Education*, Dublin: The Stationery Office.

Ireland (1990) *Report of the Primary Education Review Body*, Dublin: The Stationery Office.

Ireland (1992) *Education for a Changing World: Green paper on education*, Dublin: The Stationery Office.

Ireland (1993). *Report of the Special Education Review Committee* (SERC Report), Dublin: The Stationery Office.

Irish National Teachers Organisation (1993) *Among School Children*, Dublin: An INTO Publication.

Irish National Teachers Organisation (1994). *Remedial Education: A review*, Dublin: An INTO Publication.

Lawless, A. and Colfer, J. (1990) 'Integration: Attitudes and experiences of primary school teachers', *Reach*, 4, 1, 7–11.

Lynch, P. and MacCurtain, L. (1994) 'Resource teachers at second level: Roles, responsibilities and INSET needs', *Reach*, 8, 1, 55–64.

Lynch, P. and O'Sullivan, A. (1986) 'Remedial teaching in Irish primary schools', In Greaney, V. and Molloy, B. (eds) *Dimensions of Reading* pp.88–105). Dublin: The Educational Company.

McCormack, B. (1990) 'Pupils with a mental handicap in the ordinary school: A survey of Dublin principals', *Reach*, 4, 1, 13–18.

O'Connor, T. (1988) 'Attitudes to integration', *Reach*, 1, 2, 51–8.

Stainback, S., Stainback, W., East, K. and Sapon-Shevin (1994), 'A commentary on inclusion and the development of a positive self-identity by people with disabilities', *Exceptional Children*, 60, 6, 486–90.

CHAPTER 6

A Critical View of Integration in Italy

Irene Menegoi Buzzi

As is well known, a general law has been passed in Italy determining that all children with handicaps, regardless of the nature and seriousness of their handicaps, are to be integrated in normal/mainstream school classes. The Italian law also provides that education of the handicapped child may be pursued through a cooperation between the normal class teacher and a specialist teacher, trained to treat disabilities, who is generally defined as a 'support teacher'.

The legal regulations are applied not only to state 'compulsory' schools, which in Italy include eight grades for children and young people from 6 to 14 years; nine years ago, the integration was extended to state kindergartens (for 3–5-year-olds), for which support teachers have also been provided. The solution to the problem of integration in Italy is, therefore, a thorough and radical one. It may be conceived as the most recent phase of a long-enduring process (the origins of which may be roughly located in the late 1960s), that created a wide revision of the school system. The new outlook was based in the assumption that the final goal of education ought to be the whole, total acceptance of the disabled child in the 'normal' world.

It was difficult, almost impossible to realize, at first, the great implication that such a generalized mainstreaming hypothesis would have for the organization of whole-school curricular activities. To integrate meant to renounce definitely the principle of an exclusive competence of the school in the field of formal education. It meant imposing on all aspects of the school the heavy burden of an evaluation both of the social functions of the child, partially or wholly inhibited by the disability, and of the exploitation of the child's residual functions.

Furthermore, to integrate meant to immerse the handicapped child in the day-to-day life of the school and in the reality of every moment. It meant, at last, to place the child in a world of real motivation, to deliver him/her from the *in vitro* experience simulated within the special school, to set him/her back to a mainstream system and educational framework which might be considered akin to a normal environment, to the child's personality, age and to his/her need for self-identification and autonomy.

Naturally, this orientation towards inclusive education has led to opposition due to the political and ideological involvement of a cultural élite, that has shown its commitment to the cause of integration and a new way of conceiving social relations in community life. It was the same élite who supported the struggle against school selection according to academic evaluation, in the framework of an egalitarian pattern of human relations where academic competition had no citizenship. This élite could appeal to an explicit reference in the Italian Constitution (art.32–33) to the *right to education* for all citizens. This right was conceived as a foundation for general access to public/compulsory schools, and was interpreted as a legal sanction of the individual's possibility of self-realization in different roles according to his/her physical and intellectual potentialities. School, it was believed, should no longer be an authoritative filter of culture, but an instrument for the maintenance of personal attitudes and skills.

The pressure put on the political system by these wide changes in the general perspective of education seems to be stronger if we consider the serious crisis faced in those years by the 'special' educational institutions. The institutions were barely surviving, because they were expressions of the old centralized pattern of the Government, in contrast to administrative and political decentralization through which the Italian State had gone in the early 1970s.

The success of the movement for the revision of the law had not produced, at least in the short run, all the results which had been pursued at the beginning. As often happens, vanguards were looking at spaces located beyond the nearest obstacles in order to find a way around the situation.

They did not realize that the Italian school was not yet prepared to accept and to re-elaborate the emerging cultural issues of integration; that teachers were not given enough training and education; that there were other components in the school (such as medical, speech support, etc.); that there was still prejudice from the families of 'normal' children and reasonable doubts on the part of families of children with handicaps. Moreover, it had not been fully considered that the very school structure and internal organization had to be changed, in the following ways:

- it was no longer possible to go on with a school shaped as a mosaic of isolated classes;
- it was necessary to find times and opportunities for mixing together children of different classes and ages;
- there should not in the future be any barrier or gap between learning activities in curricular areas and expressive, recreational and play activities;
- that every teacher should transform him/herself into a social professional capable of investigating the social/educational situation of the child.

Except in some particular situations, our schools and our teachers did not seem to have the necessary prerequisites to reach these ambitious goals.

The last decade has been, therefore, almost entirely dedicated, not to the fulfilment of integration as it had been conceived in the reinterpretation of the Constitution, but to the redefinition of the planning and organization of school activities as a necessary foundation for a successful general mainstreaming of pupils with special needs.

The main decisions taken may be summarized as follows. First, changes were based on an ideological criticism of the socialization criteria for the pupils in the schools, on the ways of enforcing the laws on the *right to education*, on the evaluation of school performances, of methodological and didactic techniques and of the very contents of teaching. This review and evaluation convinced both the education and public health authorities to examine and modify the school organization which had been given the task of including children with handicaps. Hence the emphasis was on mainstreaming. In the meanwhile there was, undoubtedly, an improvement in diagnostic techniques, new theories were worked out on ways of organizing school structures and curriculum programmes, and up-to-date programmes were outlined for the decentralization of rehabilitative interventions throughout the country.

In the most recent period in Italy, public health reform has created Local Health Units (USL), which are given the responsibility for organizing facilities for safeguarding public health. At present the whole subject is under discussion, not so much on the principles as on their fulfilment. It may be interesting to consider the sub-division of tasks (between the Education Ministry and the Health Ministry) that has gradually led to a review of professional profiles.

According to the new scheme, the education of children with handicaps in public/mainstream schools has been made the responsibility of education, and is to include learning, training and socialization, whereas responsibility for re-education has been given to medical professionals.

As a result of this a new role was born within the school, the so called 'support teacher', whose task was to help the school to investigate the educational problems caused by the pupil's handicap and to carry out common work programmes for them with their peers for inclusion in the mainstream schools and currricula.

Second, there has been:

- a revision of the regulation on the evaluation of pupils and of the examination methods;
- a declaration of the right of children with handicaps to integration;
- the creation of a profile of support teachers with special qualifications;
- a reduction of the number of pupils per class;
- an emphasis on educational planning both at school and to class level as a necessary foundation for the education of children with handicaps;
- an appeal for cooperation among classes and the fulfilment of integrated and interdisciplinary activities organized by pupils belonging to the same class or to different classes (an open class system) in order to coordinate individualized didactic measures to meet the needs of individual pupils.

Third, there was the publication of a Circular letter 199.1974 which called for the collective responsibility of the school community in the aim of integrating pupils with handicaps. Also, since 1971, every prosthesis used for recovery purposes (e.g., hearing aids) is awarded free of any charge by the State.

It was only in 1983 that our Public Education Ministry circular invited the educational institutions to stipulate agreements with the rehabilitation agencies and the Local Authorities (Cirular letters 258/1983 and 250/1985).

The circular promoted the idea of similar conventions among the different authorities dealing with children with handicaps, so that they may define together, with the parents' agreement, their educational programmes and integrate their children's activities into the mainstream of the school.

By means of that circular, which until now has neither been thoroughly known nor carried into effect, the Public Education Ministry intended to promote a common planning activity extended to all the institutions and schools working in the field, including the family. Only through close cooperation and persistent follow-up of the unified programme is it possible to reach coordination of the intervention on behalf of the child, which still seems to be sectionalized (related to education or health), and often appears in contradiction to each another. These methodological prerequisites require a deep change in the very structure of the institution. If there must be coordination between the vested interests and the child's functional rehabilitation, there must also be an inter-professional link between those who are engaged in the two processes (socialization and recovery).

We may, therefore, come to the conclusion that day hospital education may be thought of as a necessary complement to re-educative activities. It may integrate, but not substitute for, the work of a specialist teacher.

Finally, a new organizational model has been established in the basis of a clear-cut division between education and rehabilitation and health functions, in spite of the overlapping nature of their functions. In the framework of such a division, two different professional qualifications have arisen, each one provided with its own objective terms of reference, and with a limited opportunity to cooperate in the pursuit of common integration aims.

It is, therefore, clear that legislative agencies as well as bureaucracy have tried to fill the gap which had arisen between the real possibilities and the initial integration purposes, because it was difficult to realize the egalitarian Utopia within the organizational reality of school. It was also problematic in relation to the quality of the school's resources and to the expectations held by society about the value of this education to the economic and productive life of the society. More particularly, there were inadequate links between the activities in the education and medical areas. This difficulty, which had its roots in the status and prestige differences between teachers and medical professionals, appeared to be serious. Beyond these incongruities and reasonable doubts about the evaluation of inclusion/mainstreaming, nobody can deny that the debate on integration has had wide repercussions throughout Italy and that the aims pursued have shown clearly that inclusion in mainstream schools has been successful.

The prerequisites of integration may be summarized as follows:

- education ought to be oriented toward the formation of the child's personality rather than toward academic selection;
- a close relationship is required between school and the social environment;

- teachers should work out and share common methodological approaches to the planning of their work;
- the turnover of teachers should be low;
- there must be a consistent methodological training on communication (with the active participation of the support teacher).

At present, all these conditions ought to be present in all schooling, including the high schools which, unlike the compulsory schools, have not yet been affected by the great changes in the State structure that have occurred in the 1970s. In the last 20 years, Parliament has been unsuccessfully debating many bills dealing with the reform of high schools, which until now remain selective and centralized institutions. They are privileged institutions and almost solely attended by pupils from the middle and upper social classes (even if less than in the past). They have few links with the social milieu in which they are physically located, and have no form of collective decision-making process. They have been neglected up to now by the laws of inclusion and mainstreaming of pupils with handicaps.

In spite of this omission, in 1988 the Ministry of Education tried to fill the gap by issuing new regulations (Circ. letter N0262/1988) according to which pupils with handicaps may be registered in a high school and may take part in its activities under the guidance of a specialist teacher. However, it must be recognized that his/her presence in the classroom normally has little influence on the methods and actual means of teaching, whereas in the compulsory schools learning levels are differentiated according to the pupils' abilities. In the high school, any pupil's performance is evaluated in a standardized and 'equal' measure and merit is judged on the basis of the student's previous academic record. In short, in the high school, students with handicaps are faced with learning problems which are typical of a selective and isolated institution.

The most recent step in the Italian legal system concerning people with handicaps is Law No 104, dated February 2 1992. This law has a very wide scope. It includes the whole spectrum of social diagnosis, from school to the world of work. The 1992 Act may be considered a fundamental law which does not introduce many innovations but tries to combine and harmonize all the pre-existing regulations in the area, making them legally binding.

As far as education is concerned, the main result of this new law may be considered the compulsory cooperation between school and health organizations: such cooperation expresses itself in the 'functional diagnosis' and in the so-called 'individualized educational plan'. The former is a thorough profile of the child with a handicap, that underlines not only the difficulties she/he meets, but tries also to highlight his/her residual recovery capabilities. The latter is a project centred in the organization of all possible support aimed at recovery and integration of the individual child into normal educational mainstream situations.

Despite all the difficulties caused by the inevitable contradictions arising from such a traditional deep cleavage, most professionals in education believe that generalized mainstreaming has been successful and that it has bought our school system to a more advanced position, even if there is still much to be done in the future.

CHAPTER 7

'Weer Samen Naar School' – a National Programme for Primary and Special Schools

Kees Den Boer

Development

While schools for the education and training of deaf and blind persons were well established in the first half of the nineteenth century, they were not financed by the Ministry of Education. In the early years of this century a small-scale system of special schools for various groups gradually emerged alongside regular education, and in 1920 the entire special education system was subsumed under the Primary Education Act. What emerged was a two-track system with separate legal arrangements for elementary and secondary education, on the one hand, and for special education on the other. Sixty-five years later this arrangement came up for major legislative review. By then the highly developed separate system had come in for severe criticism, largely on the basis of stigmatization of pupils and dubious selection criteria. The solution was an interim one– the passing of the Special Education Interim Act (ISOVSO), in 1985, designed to run for only ten years. It enabled schools to develop themselves in the direction of an 'orthopedagogical–educational institute'. The experience gleaned from this process will be used in the preparation of the 1997 legislation on special education.

Nowhere in the world can such a differentiated system of special education be found as in The Netherlands. There are 15 different types of special schools; apart from the horizontal division aimed at the special needs of the pupils there is also a vertical division aimed at the different age groups. Special infant departments for children at risk can also be attached to a number of junior special schools. Fourteen different types of secondary schools are connected to the junior special schools. Foreign visitors who have studied this system sometimes react: 'It is segregation at its best, but it is still segregation'!

The ISOVSO distinguishes the following school types for:

a) deaf children,
b) children with impaired hearing,
c) children with severe speech disorders who do not fall into groups a) or b),
d) blind children,
e) partially sighted children,
f) physically handicapped children,
g) children in hospitals,
h) chronically sick children,
i) mentally handicapped children,
j) severely mentally handicapped children,
k) severely maladjusted children,
l) children with learning and behaviour problems,
m) children in schools attached to paedogogical institutes (that is, institutes associated with a Dutch university or providing educational guidance for special schools),
n) children with multiple handicaps,
o) infants with development difficulties connected to schools which fall into group i), k) or l).

Severely mentally handicapped children (generally IQ range approximately 30 to 50) who have additional serious problems and children who are functioning below this level are not in schools. They usually live in residential settings and are not the responsibility of the education authorities.

Placement of a pupil in a special school is possible only after assessment by a board of experts. The composition of this board may differ for every type of school, but in all cases the principal of the school and a representative of regular/mainstream education are members, as also are a psychologist, a doctor and a social worker. The board of experts records its conclusions in a joint report and the principal of the school is obliged to discuss its conclusions with them. Two years after admittance the pupil must be reassessed.

Education in a special school must follow a schoolwork plan (SWP), which is developed by the teachers and the other educational experts in the school team and requires the approval of the board of governors every two years. Apart from this SWP, which has been obligatory since 1987, every school has to adopt an activity plan based on the plan, describing the daily routine of the educational process. The school and/or the teacher may also develop educational plans which embody programmes for individual pupils or for certain categories of pupils. In response to criticism of segregation, the Interim Act sanctioned two developments. The first of these was designed to make special schools less restricted to categories of handicap.

For the future, an Advisory Council for Primary and Special Education proposes the following categories:

Category 1: Schools for children with delayed development, children with learning disabilities, children with learning and behaviour problems.
Category 2: Schools for children with very specific special educational needs (for example, physically handicapped and multiply handicapped children).
Category 3: Schools for children who need support during their whole life (for example children who are severely mentally retarded).

Category 1

The Act '*weer samen naar school*' ('together to school'– mainstream education as a common responsibility of primary schools and special schools), which was introduced by the Lower House of The Netherlands government, is intended to bring together the schools for children with learning and behaviour problems and to extend them into regional support centres.

In addition to teaching, it is the support centre's task to accompany children with handicaps at primary schools as well as providing advice for staff within the school. Moreover, the procedure of placing a pupil in a special school is now carried out by central committees and not as before by school-bound committees.

In view of the planned changes, the headteachers of the participating special schools have amalgamated into a syndicate that warns, at expert conferences and through publication, not to translate the reforms into action too rapidly.

Category 2

Concerning the schools belonging to this category, there has been no official documentation yet. However, on the basis of the present developments the following tendencies emerge:

- The schools for blind and partially sighted children develop into school communities, usually with boarding schools, for those pupils who could not be supported in schools in spite of all possible help.
- The integration of schools for deaf children and children with impaired hearing, which is causing problems because sign language is the focus of the schools for deaf children, while schools for children with impaired hearing prefer verbal/oral approaches to language learning and communication. An additional problem is the unclassified situation of the schools for children with speech disorders.
- The schools for physically handicapped children have much experience concerning the support of physically handicapped children at primary schools. In this area it is not clear whether children with severe handicaps should go to school or, as before, be supported in day care centres.
- The Netherlands' schools for educational support, for children in hospitals and pedagogical institute schools, will develop to support diagnostic centres for children with psychological problems.

Category 3

The schools for children who are severely mentally retarded will go on with their development, which is child-centred and oriented to the Russian psychology of learning theory.

Collaboration with the schools in category 2 and the primary schools will come to the fore. In this context, one can see the efforts being made for the integration of children with Downs Syndrome; there are currently 230 such children attending mainstream primary schools. Corresponding claims made by the parent's association of mentally handicapped children support and reinforce this development of inclusive practices.

Current provision

In order to comprehend the reform process in The Netherlands, two particular aspects are to be mentioned. In contrast to other countries, there was no substantial integration movement from 'below', neither on the part of the respective parents nor on the part of the teachers. Additionally, the fact that free school choice is established by the Constitution has scarcely had any effect on the extension of inclusive provision in the schooling of children and young people with handicaps and learning difficulties so far. Approximately 95 per cent of children with special educational needs in the age group 4–12 still attend a special school.

The attempt to change the current conditions and to shift the special educational competence to the regular/mainstream school and above all, the 8-year primary school, is initiated by the responsible authorities of The Netherlands government. Financial considerations play an important role, as does the preservation of the particularly differentiated special educational system, in contrast to the desire to reduce, in the long run, the selection in schools and the related isolation of pupils with handicaps and learning difficulties.

General aims of the programme

The governments' programme, '*weer samen naar school*' (together to school) intends to bring to the fore the common responsibility of primary schools and special schools for children with learning difficulties. Within the framework of this project the schools for children with learning disabilities, for children with learning and behaviour problems and for children with delayed development covers approximately 72 per cent of the special schools. All the other types of special schools are concerned only a to a small extent.

It is a matter of developing a common support framework for pupils with special educational needs, in order to bind together the primary school and the special school more closely. There is agreement about the special education system being able to provide help early, quickly and flexibly to children with learning and development problems at the regular schools. The common responsibility for continuous support must replace the current systematic separation of special schools and regular schools. At the same time, this means the creation of a legal, organizational and pedagogical-didactic framework which makes it possible that children with special educational needs can be supported through their schooling individually and flexibly.

The first version of the government programme was both revolutionary and radical. In order to enforce the common responsibility of regular schools and special schools for children with special educational needs, the govermnent proposed to abolish the direct financing of special schools and to spread these funds over to the regular/mainstream schools for the support of pupils with special educational needs. In this way the special educational expertise would be shifted into the regular school and thus stop the competition between the different special schools. By spreading the funds and with the help of all the support systems from the special schools, the regular school should develop into an institution which can do justice to every child.

After discussion in Parliament and in the professional associations and institutions, not much has remained of this radical proposal. Common mainstream classes are still the aim, but the existence of special schools has not been relinquished. The present situation indicates again the 'as well as' policy. On the one hand, distinctly more children with handicaps and disadvantages should be taught in the regular school; on the other, the special schools for children with learning and behaviour difficulties (category 1 schools) are basically preserved.

However, it appears that the new way forward is to see the special school system developing into special educational consultancy centres for the regular school system. Moreover, it is laid down that the number of pupils attending a special school must not exceed the level existing before January 1992. The central question is, in which direction the pendulum will swing until 1997? Currently it is not possible to carry through the original idea of common classes as the aim and means for greater inclusion in Dutch schools.

There are no common future prospects for those with the political will for inclusion and those who are affected at the level of the school. These prospects are not being achieved because recent attempts have shown little success. Moreover, scientists such as the school sociologist Doornbos (1991), hint again and again at the fact that the growing number of pupils attending a special school is less a problem of the special schools themselves, but that the reason is more likely to be found in the permanent excessive demands on the primary school. Without a radical change, particularly in the resource-supply conditions under which the primary school has to work, it cannot meet its task to be a school for all children and thus is forced to keep its selective function.

Mainstream education as a common responsibility of primary schools and special schools

The innovation programme '*weer samen naar school*' is a country-wide project. Affected are 8,300 primary schools, 289 collaboration associations of primary and special schools, 66 peripatetic school support services, 40 institutions of initial teacher training for the primary sector, three training institutes for special educational teachers, additional country-wide acting institutions (for example for curriculum development, for the assessment system, for school and lesson research), organizations of governing bodies, teacher unions, organizations of parents and the Ministry of Education.

Additionally, there are the institutions of school management, school book publishers, the children and young persons as well as the universities involved. It is the aim of the project to motivate the involved groups of people and institutes towards a responsible collaboration in order to turn the primary school into an appropriate place for children with special educational needs in the long run. On the one hand, the great autonomy of The Netherlands' education system and the involved competition between the institutions represents an immense obstacle for this marathon trial. On the other hand, this autonomy gives the opportunity, in connection with the common desire to change, to develop solutions which are regionally specific and oriented towards the needs of the pupils, teachers and institutions.

It is agreed that the change started with the headteachers. It is obvious from recent research that about 73 per cent of the parents of 4 – 12-year-olds are in favour of the integration of special educational expertise into primary schools. Only 10 per cent of the parents are still of the opinion that special schools for children with handicaps are essential (Appelhof, 1993). There is consensus that the enormous changes which are due to be dealt with, can only be put through by the affected persons themselves. The setting-up of collaborative associations is a substantial instrument to enable this to happen. The fact that this initiative was not enforced by the schools or parents themselves still remains problematical.

A collaborative association consists of one or more special schools in category I and a large number of primary schools. A collaboration contract is worked out by all the involved schools and authorities concerned to form the basis for a collaboration unit. A network of centres throughout the country is planned so that every primary school in The Netherlands is connected to an association. Presently there are about 290 collaborative associations, which comprise nearly all primary schools and special schools. The number of pupils per collaborative unit varies enormously, ranging between 1,000 and 10,000 pupils. It is striking that 72 per cent of the collaboration centres are not 'pillar-formed', i.e. they don't correspond to the existing three pillars: 'Catholic, Protestant or public'. The financial funds per collaborative association vary according to the number of pupils and the number of special schools involved. Twenty-eight Dutch Guilders are made available per pupil and 5,000 Dutch Guilders per special school. The funds are tied to the purpose of the development and provision of special educational support, including material resources and personnel. Thus, all in all, 90,000 Dutch Guilders are made available for a centre with 3,000 primary pupils and one special school. For the moment, this regulation runs for two years. If, in spite of this, the number of pupils at special schools continues to rise, the funds for the '*weer samen naar school*' programme will be cut.

The award of the financial grant depends on two conditions: 1. the participation in a collaboration association; 2. the development of an extensive support programme. Each collaborative association has to set forth within the framework of this support programme which educational programmes are provided for children with development difficulties and children with learning and behaviour problems in order to support them at the primary school. Additionally, there must be a detailed representation about the use of the financial funds which are related to this. Thus, the educational programmes are established on three levels:

1. at the school and institution (comprehensive) level referring to the collaborative associations;
2. at the individual school level; and
3. at the level of single learning groups and classes.

The attempt to avoid 'school failure' at the primary school by appropriate and individual means, to reduce the number of transfers to special schools and to realize the integration of handicapped and non-handicapped children, is seen as the central task of primary teachers. To support the associations and to strengthen their position is the focus of success in integration. Moreover, the individual school is understood, to an increasing degree, as a 'learning organization', in which common learning and teaching are a permanent process of development, which is supported by the collaborative associations.

To respond to the excessive demands on teachers and their often mentioned need for training to support the education of pupils with special educational needs, many collaborative centres have developed 'internal consultancy systems'. One aspect of the system is the establishment of '*Orthotheken*'. An '*Orthothek*' includes the technical literature for the inclusion/integration work, tests and games for the observation of behaviour, different kinds of supporting material which can be used in lessons, didactically prepared material for the individual support of reading, writing and maths, as well as a list containing the addresses of all possible collaboration partners.

A further element are the learning development reports for every pupil (*leerlingenvolgsystem*) and the pedagogical conferences as a means of discussing these reports (*leerlingenbesprekingen*). The establishment of an internal consultancy teacher is considered to be very important. This is a teacher from the corresponding primary school team, whose task it is to coordinate the resources and curriculum support concerning the children with special educational needs who are included. His/her teaching load will be temporarily suspended for the time necessary. Furthermore, s/he is in charge of the '*Orthothek*'; s/he has to keep it up to date and has to provide direct consultancy and support to the staff in the school. Additionally, there is the collaboration with institutions outside the school as well as the normal administrative tasks linked with school life.

The internal consultancy teachers are trained within the framework of accompanying continuing studies, which take two years. They are specially trained in communication and consultancy techniques but also in spelling support, maths support and behaviour observation. According to the size of the school and the number of pupils the time allowed for the internal consultancy varies, up to that necessary for a full-time job. A range of collaborative associations also provide regular meetings and supervision help and advice for the consultancy teachers.

Support for the mainstream primary teachers is provided by school internal 'remedial teachers' and by 'peripatetic teachers' (special educationalists). Remedial teachers are, as the internal consultancy teachers, members of the primary school team and are specialized in the area of diagnosis and individual learning support through appropriate continuing studies. The focus of their work is the observation of individual children with learning and/or behaviour problems within the class; they must also help the class teacher with the development of individual support programmes. The work of the 'consultancy teacher' is likely to be based at the school level generally, whereas the remedial teachers' task focuses on individual pupil and teacher support.

Peripatetic teachers are professional teachers from neighbouring special schools. They offer specific support for children with physical handicaps and their primary school teachers. Additionally, peripatetic support is provided for those children who are transferred to a primary school after having attended a school for children with learning disabilities or for maladjusted children for at least one year. This form of peripatetic support is provided for no more than one school year. Because of the previous very strict separation of special schools and primary schools, there is little experience of this kind of collegial support in The Netherlands.

To sum up, at present the activities within the framework of the '*weer samen naar school*' innovation in The Netherlands are predominantly in the area of the constitution and development of collaborative associations. The work of the internal consultancy teachers, the remedial and peripatetic consultancy teachers has just started and the respective means of continuing development and support for teachers is established. However, it will take some years before the results of these innovations, which can be used for research and analysis, will be available.

Before we come to a final evaluation of the innovation process, one project should explain the more theoretical aspects of what has been described.

This project has been running for more than 10 years and is analysed by researchers, who are not themselves involved in this project. The following example explains the work of a collaboration association in Opsterland in the north of The Netherlands.

Opsterland

Opsterland is a big, rural state community in the south-east of Friesland with a very high unemployment rate. In the 16 villages of the district there are 28 public and Protestant primary schools. Each school has between 70 and 100 pupils and thus less than the average of the country; they are small rural primary schools.

Figure 7.1 Percentage of children transferred to special education, 1975–1990

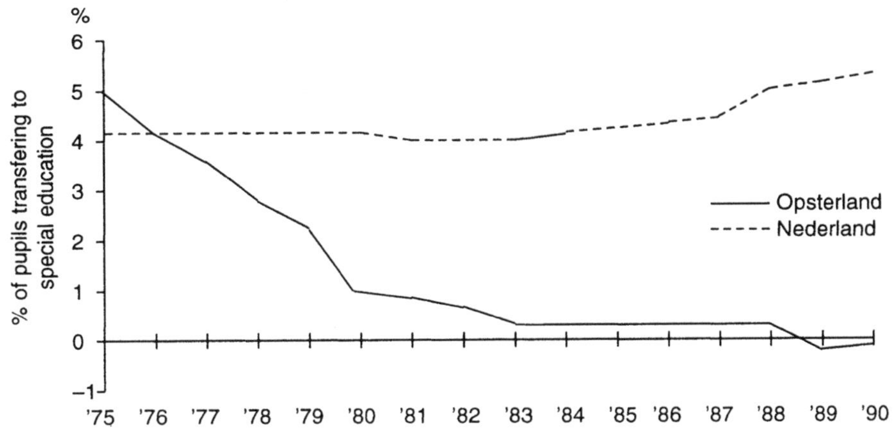

(*Source*: Bergman and Bouma, 1991)

During recent years, the primary schools have developed through a successful collaborative association so that few children had to be transferred to special schools, as Figure 7.1 shows. It can be seen that the number of children transferring to special educational placements has decreased dramatically between 1975 and 1990. From a situation where 5 per cent of children were referred to special schools, in recent years we can see from the negative percentage of –1 per cent that transfers from special schools to mainstream schools are more likely in this new situation. This has come about as a result of liaison between the schools and the respective school consultancy service. In addition to the consultancy and information function of the consultancy service, its importance in the role of collaboration is emphasized.

The aims and content of the collaboration are designed by the school's headteachers through regular established meetings arranged with the respective school teams. With the help of the peripatetic service, the decisions worked out about pupils in agreement with the school teams are then translated into action. In this way it has been possible, in recent years, to achieve a good match with respect to consultancy and support on the one hand and the reality of the school work for individual pupils on the other. This is unique – even for the conditions in The Netherlands.

It is the common aim of the primary schools in Opsterland to ensure an optimal development for all of their residential school pupils. This is guaranteed by means of:

- the development of a common school pedagogy and organization,
- the professionalization of teachers,
- differentiated materials and curriculum for children with delayed development and learning and behaviour problems.

The high efficiency of the Opsterlander schools is based on the permanent interplay of independent possibilities for each school to take their own action, on the transfer of expertise between the schools, on the support provided by the peripatetic service and the educational support for the individual pupil which is collaboratively designed.

The high motivation for the school collaboration has been established because of the realization that individual schools cannot manage to become a 'school for all' children and cannot solve their 'integrational' problems without help.

Within the framework of the support of children with special educational needs, the schools act on the basis of a common model. At every school there is a 'remedial teacher' whose working hours are determined according to the size of the school. If there are any problems for individual children, the class teacher responsible will bring the conversation around to these problems at the pedagogical meeting. The 'remedial teacher' observes the individual child in the learning group and carries out the necessary diagnostic examination. The conclusions are recorded in a report and are discussed at the team meetings. A collaborative individual educational plan is developed for the child and this plan is translated into action by the class teacher and/or the remedial teacher. During the support phase, a 'log book' is used and the educational methods are evaluated after three months. If there are any changes or developments concerning the respective pupil after this period of time, the peripatetic service is asked for support. In addition to the general teachers and the subject teachers (*Fachlebrer*), a 'special' teacher is also involved in providing this service.

The model of Opsterland emphasizes the importance of the individual school and its joint action in the framework of the innovation process. It also shows that the support by other schools and the peripatetic service represents an essential help and relief for the individual school as well as for the teachers involved.

The concentration of specialist expertise and the associated quality improvement of the primary schools serve all the pupils in the schools, and in particular the children with disadvantages and handicaps.

References

Appelhof, P. N., (1993) 'Onderwijskundige implicaties van het Weer Samen Naar School – beleid', in Parneyer N.K. (Hrsg) *Weer Samen Naar School...op weg naar 1997*, Assen.

Bergman, J.W. and Bouma, R. (1991) 'Samen naar school in Opsterland', in Doornbos (op.cit.). Doornbos, K. (1991) *Samen naar school. Aangepast onderwijs in gewone scholen*, Nijkerk.

CHAPTER 8

Inclusive Schools in Portugal

Ana Maria Benard da Costa

Introduction

When writing an account of 'inclusive schools', some basic questions need to be faced. Are there inclusive schools in Portugal? If so, how important is inclusive education in the school system as a whole, and when and where did the inclusive school tendency start?

According to the fundamental principle of the 'inclusive school', which is that 'all children should learn together, wherever possible, regardless of any difficulties or differences they may have' (Draft Framework for Action on Special Needs Education, Salamanca World Conference, 1994), we have to conclude that to answer these questions is very difficult or even impossible.

If the aim of this account was to describe the 'integration' of disabled students in regular schools, we could rely on the different data traditionally mentioned in this context i.e., the number of students enrolled in the different schools divided by their category of disability, number of resource teachers, existence of other professionals specially appointed to support them and different school and related support systems. The different approaches adopted until now in 'integrated education' – withdrawal, remedial and mainstreaming (Ainscow, 1991) – can be described through the objective measures involved, concerning the children previously considered, as having some kind of disability or a certain special educational need.

But if we try to describe schools which attempt to teach 'all children', improving school organization and teaching methods in order to enable them to reach the maximum possible success, we cannot find any landmarks to facilitate our research: previous assessments and student classifications, number of hours of tutoring, number and types of support systems, etc. In this case we are looking for pointers of a more subtle and subjective nature which are not revealed through this kind of information; we are talking about attitudes, about expectations, about teaching methods, about classroom atmosphere, about school environments. And we know that some of the most important events in this field are taking place in the intimacy of regular classrooms, unknown outside the school and the student's family environment. Only a complete and complex survey could permit an insight into this reality, and this survey has not, so far, been carried out in Portugal.

Concerning the question of timing and location – where and when this inclusive tendency started – the difficulties in answering this are just as great. We know the dates of the more important legal measures concerning this approach and we can pinpoint the places where some innovative programmes took place but, once more, we cannot underestimate the role of so many other teachers and schools which, over the years, has permitted a successful regular school achievement to students with special needs. We have the testimony of some handicapped adults who revealed to us their experience of real inclusion, at a time when this expression – as well as 'school integration' or even 'special education' – was almost unknown.

Nevertheless, attempting at least to arrive at a rough perspective on this matter, we will underline those measures which can be considered as landmarks in the long transition from an exclusive to an inclusive orientation in education in Portugal.

At the risk of making a very unrepresentative selection, we will choose some schools which we think are close to this inclusive approach, and will try to describe their strategies and their struggle to cope with the different individual needs of their pupils.

The first steps towards school integration

Since the inception of a National Educational System, and since schools moved from being intended exclusively for a restricted élite, there have been pupils with special educational needs – in particular, learning difficulties – in regular/mainstream classes. Until the beginning of this decade the common strategy for coping with them consisted in having them repeat the grade. Very often the difficulties persisted, and another repetition followed. The percentage of repetition was different from school to school (many studies have been published explaining the most important variables connected with this factor) but the figures varied between 20 per cent to 40 per cent of all pupils. Most critical were the early grades: children could remain in this phase till they reached the age of 14. Then they were removed from this type of school and, in some cases, could attend a night class.

If the child had some kind of severe disability, the possibility of acceptance in a regular school was considered neither by the school directors nor by the parents themselves. There were exceptions to this attitude, but these were isolated cases relying, mostly, on the direct intervention of a parent as no kind of educational support was available. The law specifically stated that these pupils could be exempted from school if their disability was testified by a doctor and alternative educational programmes were not specified.

In the mid-1960s, a first attempt to change this situation was made. A group of blind and visually disabled students were accepted into a regular/mainstream secondary school and, for the first time, a resource teacher was appointed to support this integrated programme. Other schools followed this initiative and, by the end of the decade, with the assistance of support teachers freshly trained in this field, many students with severe visual problems were accepted in regular classes. This programme was directly supported by the intervention of the Welfare Department (which provided the support teacher and the special materials) with the Ministry of Education remaining in a very passive role.

The first legal measures in the educational sector concerning the education of children with disabilities in regular schools, integrated on a full- or part-time basis in regular classes, were established in the mid-1970s, as part of an important educational reform.

Through this reform were created, at a central level, under the Departments for Compulsory and Secondary Education, Special Education Divisions, and, at a local level, Special Educational Teams, composed mainly of resource teachers. These Teams strove towards family, social and school integration for children with sensorial and motor disabilities, with each resource teacher supporting different students spread around different schools, sometimes with considerable distances between them.

In 1975 the first Decree was published concerning the integration of students with disabilities, establishing the support measures to be organized by the regular schools. The most important of these was the possibility of individual tutoring given by regular teachers and the possibility of using special materials and different forms of communication, used either during instruction or in the final evaluation. To be entitled to these benefits, the students needed a medical prescription testifying to the existence of one or more disabilities.

The different initiatives which took place during the first steps towards school integration were governed by the following principles:

- the support was totally child-centred, aiming to remediate existing disabilities through direct intervention using the special resources or the regular teacher;
- students with disabilities admitted in regular schools were to be able to follow – if necessary through some special instruction methods – the common curriculum, and it was clearly laid down that their presence in the regular classroom should not entail any fundamental changes or any kind of disturbance to the 'non-disabled' students;
- the administrative and financial measures needed were to come almost entirely from the resource teacher and the Special Education Departments; the regular school was in no way responsible for these matters;
- the parents were not asked to participate in the decisions concerning the special programmes planned for their children.

During this decade, a growing number of regular/mainstream schools have encountered pupils that until then had been exclusively confined to their homes or to special centres. Among others, children diagnosed as blind, deaf or hard of hearing, physically or neurologically impaired, have been enrolled in primary or secondary schools all over the country and the former negative attitudes from the school directors or from the teachers have started to change.

We can consider these first steps as signifying a breakthrough, having set in motion the debate (which is continuing today) on attitudes towards education, the role of regular teachers and the importance of mainstream education in the future social and professional integration of people with disabilities.

Nevertheless, by the beginning of the 1980s, the influence received from available literature (The Warnock Report, published in the UK in 1978, has been especially important), awareness of developments in this field during the 1970s in many other countries and, especially, the Portuguese experience itself, had contributed to some fundamental changes which led to the next phase in the process towards school inclusion.

The second phase: school integration of students with special educational needs

We can describe this second phase through some of the landmarks which have contributed, in different ways, towards the evolution of the situation mentioned above.

1. The inclusion of students with moderate and severe learning problems in the group of those supported by the 'Special Education Teams'.

This event can be considered a major step, as it profoundly changed the existing conceptual principles. A student with this kind of educational need cannot participate in a normal class, even on a part-time basis, without requiring an active intervention from the regular teacher and a curriculum adaptation. In order to 'integrate' these students, measures such as the support of the resource teacher, individual tutoring or the assignment of special materials were not sufficient. Their presence questioned, in some cases, the whole school organization, from timetables to architecture, from classroom management to instruction methods, and it implied, always, the active contribution from school directors and educational staff.

On the other hand, the organization of the Special Educational Teams and the 'itinerant' work of most of its members had to undergo a profound change, as a much closer link between the special resource teacher and the schools was needed. Support teachers were asked into the regular schools on a full-time basis, and their link with the school became stronger as their link with the Teams became weaker.

2. The evolution of the policy concerning school integration: from the support given to students with different categories of disability (sensorial, physical or mental disabled) to the support given to 'special needs students'.

This evolution is linked with many factors:

- the integration in regular schools of students with learning difficulties (mentioned above);
- the influence of international recommendations concerning 'Education for All';
- the literature concerning this approach.

The combined effect of these factors (among many others) produced a profound change in the attitudes of regular school staff and of the 'special education services', at a central, regional and local level. Instead of focusing exclusively on students previously designated as having a specific disability, resource teachers were asked to work with a much larger population, including children with 'difficulties in school'. The resource teacher was no longer considered responsible only for the support of those cases having a 'visible' sensorial or physical problem but also for those who had difficulties in learning due to a great variety of reasons.

The former strategy of the 'special education teams', based on a child-centred approach and functioning principally by means of intervention in a separate resource room, was called into question and, in some schools, was substituted by other methods: support inside the regular classroom, participation of regular teachers (and not only the 'special teacher'), reorganization of some school activities, etc. At the same time, the responsibility of regular schools concerning students with special needs increased.

3. The development in the support system of three new perspectives.

These new perspectives were:

- the substitution of medical prescription concerning the provision of special education measures with educational and psychological reports;
- the attention given to the parent's opinions concerning assessment and delivery of special educational provisions for their children;
- the establishment of 'individual educational plans' as guidelines for all school intervention.

4. Legislation

In Portugal, legislation governing the education of children with special needs has tended to follow, rather than initiate, new developments. Its major role has been to consolidate and strengthen the new approaches and, in some cases, to guarantee the supply of material resources.

Three important laws dating from the 1980s and the early 1990s must be mentioned:

> The Basic Law for Education (1986) which mentions the right of all children with disabilities to be educated and the priority given to their education in normal/mainstream schools.

> The law concerning the obligation for all children, including those with severe disabilities, to be included in compulsory education (Decree no 3 5/90).
>
> The law establishing the different measures which must be available in regular schools, in order to answer to the special education needs of their students (Decree no 319/91).

This legislation meant that, for the first time, the education of these students ceased to be 'a welfare matter' and become the responsibility of the Educational Department. The translation of those principles into real practice is still an ongoing process, and is far from having reached its established objectives.

Considering the importance of Decree no 319/91 in the practices introduced in the school system in order to accommodate students with special needs, we will describe briefly, its fundamental points:

- the school must be a 'school for all', being responsible for the education of students having disabilities or learning difficulties;
- in order to cope with the special educational needs which some students may have, the schools shall undertake different 'special education measures' according to each individual situation;
- the 'special education measures' can be of an administrative, curricular or organizational nature (individual support, adapted or alternative curricula, individualized timetable, use of special equipment, utilization of special means of communication);
- in order to be eligible for one or more special educational measures, there is the need for a proposal presented by the school psychologist and the teachers, as well as written agreement from the parents;
- the special education measures must be established in an 'individual educational plan', which must be signed by the parents and by the members of staff concerned with the student.

This phase, which we have just briefly described, is still prevalent in most schools but a gradual transition is taking place. We will now attempt to outline the changes taking place in some schools, bearing in mind that this is a difficult task, since the symptoms of these changes have not yet been analysed and the examples of this tendency are still very limited.

The emerging 'inclusive schools' phase

As has already been mentioned, changes in educational processes and in the attitudes of the educators do not follow legislation; on the contrary, they are the prerequisites for amendments to the law. During the 1990s, the presence of students with severe learning difficulties in many schools – this number has been growing rapidly each year – has produced in many school educational teams the need to rethink their teaching strategies and to reform the whole educational system. The traditional approach of 'individual extra support' has started to be questioned and the role of the 'special teacher' has been profoundly rethought. In some schools, the support teacher has moved from the separate resource room to the regular class, working side by side with the regular teacher, with both sharing responsibility for the class in order to permit a more individualized instruction; in other schools, students with very severe or multiple disabilities have stayed based in a special class but an interaction with non-disabled peers has been developed through various strategies; finally, in other situations, a fundamental change in the whole school system is being initiated which aims to permit the development of project-based and group-based activities.

In many of these schools the pertinent questions have been: 'If we are doing our best to facilitate access to the curriculum to our students with severe learning difficulties, how can we accept that those having much less severe school problems are failing to learn?' and, 'What can we do to reach the needs of each child or young person?'

This evolution of ideas, of strategies and of educational options is just starting, in some cases within the school environment, and in other cases at a district or regional level with the support of some educational leaders.

The development of this tendency faces, nevertheless, great difficulties: lack of know-how in adopting different teaching strategies, organizational barriers, especially at post-elementary level, lack of educational materials, etc. For the majority of the schools to be considered 'schools for all', a great change must be undertaken in many fields: in school administration, in teacher recruitment, in educational support for teachers and, especially, in teacher training. We can say that, in Portugal, as in most countries, the 'inclusive school' is still a 'Utopia' belonging to the future. Nevertheless we can mention some schools which are already very close to this perspective and which are progressing rapidly towards this 'Utopian' goal.

We are now going to talk about some of these schools. They were not singled out from a national survey; they are simply some schools among many others which try to provide the best opportunities for all the children of their community.

Two primary schools in the city of Espinho

Espinho is a coastal town in the North of Portugal with a population of about 23,000. It has a large beach and during summer is a popular holiday resort. Apart from tourism, its activities consist of various industries, commerce, services and fishing.

The *Marinha Elementary School* is located in one of the poorest neighbourhoods, a fishing community with very severe economic, social, cultural and moral problems and where children present a general very low school achievement. 'The main difficulty was that children did not want to come to school and that they had a very high rate of school failure', said the school principal.

The school has about 100 students, all of them from the surrounding area, divided into pre-school and elementary classes from first to fourth grade. In the same grade we can find children of different ages, which is explained by the high rate of failures.

In 1991/92, the director of the local school district, together with the leader of the local special education team decided to organize a 'remedial classroom' to provide extra educational support to children with learning difficulties. A support teacher was appointed and a special room was supplied. She started to work with students (selected by the teachers or by a school psychologist) in small groups, for some hours a week. It was supposed, at the beginning, that this remedial room would follow the traditional pattern of so many others spread all around the country: children would go there to receive some individualized remedial help in academic matters, in the hope that, afterwards, they would perform better in the regular class.

However, as the support teacher became aware of the children's situation, of the very deprived conditions of their lives and of their reluctance to attend school, she realized that merely giving some extra schooling would not be an effective solution. Children would hate to attend the resource room as much as they hated to attend the regular classes. 'I tried to reach them through others ways: by evaluating their capacities, and the knowledge they already had, concentrating on events which they could relate to because they were near to their own experiences, and create in the space a homely atmosphere, different from the classroom environment', the resource teacher told me. The principal was asked to spend more money than usual on bird cages, plants, tissues, clay, painting materials, small musical instruments, large sheets of paper, etc. The starting point for the activities was always suggested by the children: a party was being prepared in the neighbourhood, a new fishing boat had just arrived; a visit to the market, were some of the projects.

At the beginning of the school year a major storm hit the coast and several fishing families' houses were flooded by sea water. This was an important event reported in the local and national newspapers and was an excellent opportunity for a collective study: newspaper surveys, interviews with people whose houses were damaged, researching in geography books on storms, etc. All this information was collected through many means (writing, drawings, collage of newspaper articles, etc.) in a large dossier which was presented directly to the Mayor of the town. In reply, he visited the school and spent some time with the students.

This room was, initially, still known as the 'remedial room' and only students previously selected would attend it, for some hours a week. After some time, the name changed, signifying a change in its nature: it became the 'school resource room' used by the resource teacher and the regular teachers in many ways, Students, in small groups, would receive support and individualized attention, larger groups would work on different projects, and some children having other school difficulties or greater emotional problems, would come on a regular basis.

One of the most important changes to have occurred in the school has been the interaction between teachers and parents. As the projects were connected with the environment where the children lived and involved their family and neighbours, this interaction was, very often, asked for. Parents lost their distance or even their fear concerning the school and the school staff and started to consider it as a place where they could find understanding and, in many cases, support. Problems related with child neglect or, in some cases, with child abuse, did not disappear completely but, in many situations, the parent-children relationships improved considerably.

The evaluation carried out at the end of this school year showed a enormous decrease in absenteeism and a significant improvement in learning by most of the students. These results led the school staff to undertake another step, consisting of applying the same teaching methods in the various regular classrooms. Instead of considering the activities described above as 'free-time activities', conducted side by side with the curricular ones, this school is beginning to change traditional school methods and to adopt the educational perspective which was introduced in the school resource room.

Some of the teachers are insecure and feel that they would need training to work in such a different way to the one they are used to. Responding to this need, a time for discussion and interaction between the regular teacher and the resource teacher is planned before the start of the next school year.

This school is, certainly, not providing the best of opportunities to all students. There is still a long way to go to reach that aim. Nevertheless, it is a school that has improved immensely in this sense and where children have discovered that learning is possible, that working together can be fun and that discovering and knowing can be exciting.

Some time ago most of these children felt helpless about succeeding, faced frustration at every lesson and reacted through various forms of misbehaviour. Some space, a few materials, but, essentially, a new educational approach, have made possible the profound change in their 'school life' and in the 'life of the school' which we have tried briefly to describe.

The *Anta Elementary School* comprises a middle-class population in a central neighbourhood of the town. It has a modern building designed for an 'open school' programme and, like the Marinha School has about 100 students from pre-school to fourth grade.

In the school year of 1991/92, the parents of one child with severe learning problems and the parents of another child with motor and mental disabilities caused by cerebral palsy, living nearby, asked for their enrolment in the school. The children had received support during a former stay in a Day Care Centre and their files containing the result of developmental and psychological assessment were presented to the school principal. It was the first time that this school was confronted with children with such severe problems and their first reaction was to try to send them to a special school due to the lack of necessary resources.

The Special Education Regional Office had developed a policy concerning students with severe handicaps which consisted of keeping them in regular schools, sometimes in small groups with the support of special staff and with different kinds of materials and special administrative measures. Acting on this policy, the leader of the local special education team proposed to the school staff the organization of a special class for these children, assuring the collaboration of a special teacher, an assistant teacher and the cooperation of a psychologist and a physiotherapist from a local special school. This meant that other severely disabled children would be able to share these facilities.

These were the first steps in a process which, since then, have given rise to a profound modification of the structure of this school and its educational goals. We will try to describe briefly its current policy and practice.

The Anta School proclaims the right for every child from its geographical area to be accepted as a student, no matter what the existing disabilities he or she may have, and opens its doors to other severely disabled children from all around the city, up to approximately ten. For the moment, there are seven students with a variety of multiple dysfunction: cerebral palsy, 'Cornelio de Lange' Syndrome, microcephalia and brain damage, among others. Three are non-verbal and were not toilet trained when they started school; one, at the beginning of the school year, had no form of communication and is just starting to express some forms of body communication; one girl has severe learning problems but as she is able to participate in several activities in the regular class, she will be integrated, next year, in most of the day schedule. One boy with cerebral palsy has very severe motor problems and cannot talk, but has a high level of intelligence and can communicate through a computer. This student is fully integrated in the regular fourth grade, successfully following the common curriculum.

The class includes an extra teacher who supplies the needed support to this student and cooperates with the whole class in a more individualized approach.

In order to meet to the severe special needs of these children, the following human and material resources have been organized in the school:

- one special teacher and two assistant teachers;
- a special class with special educational materials designed to improve motor and mental development;
- specially adapted bathrooms;
- ramps in place of stairs;
- means of transport.

The reason why I selected this elementary school is not related to the existence of a special class for severely disabled children or the fact that a pupil with multiple handicaps is in a regular class on a full-time basis We can find, nowadays, several instances of this situation all around the country. This selection is related, basically, to the particular conditions surrounding this integration, which I will try to describe next.

The presence of students with disabilities has been matter for profound reflection for all school staff as they have assumed that the former were full-time students and should be involved as much as possible in all school activities. This attitude was also adopted by most of the students and, after initial reluctance, was shared by the parents. If it was obvious that some of these students needed to spend some time in the special class and receive there some specific training, it was also decided that the school should organize different activities which could be easily shared by them. The decision was to organize, all around the school year, active participation in the national and local festivities, using them as motives for projects carried in different directions. Christmas, Halloween, the City-Saint-Day, Carnival, etc., became the themes for parties, theatrical performances, exhibitions, study visits, etc. All these activities were designed in such a way that all children with disabilities could participate, when necessary with the direct help of their non-disabled peers.

Through these initiatives, educational strategies have improved considerably, with positive results for all students. Some of those having moderate learning difficulties have developed interest and motivation in school; others with behaviour problems felt responsible for cooperation with their disabled school-mates and their attitudes have changed considerably.

Between the regular and the special class, close cooperation has been established and not only do most of the students with disabilities spend time in the regular classes, but the special class is used by all as a resource room where they come to participate in activities such as art, computers, or home economics.

This interchange has signified the global participation of all the members of the staff in the programme, which is no longer considered as a 'matter for the special teacher' or belonging to the 'special education sector'. The change in attitudes and of policy, from the 'integration of special needs' to 'the inclusive school', can be demonstrated in this school. The barriers between classes, children and staff have faded away; we can see, instead, a close and rich interaction between children and adults in a common effort to give to each one the maximum opportunities for development. In order to implement this project in the coming year, regular class teachers and the resource teacher are together looking for the best ways to respond to each student with a disability according to individual needs, and finding his or her ways to bring about their participation in regular classes.

The preparatory school in the city of S. Pedro do Sul

Before referring to the experiment carried out in this school, it is important to give some information about the organization of a 'preparatory school' in Portugal.

Preparatory schools receive students who have finished elementary school, and go from 5th grade until the end of compulsory basic education, at 9th grade. In these schools the system of subject teaching begins: a different teacher is responsible for each school subject, having classes of 50 minutes, at various times each week. At grade 5 the students start with six curriculum matters and they reach nine subjects at grade 9. Some time is left for the school to organize intercurricular project work.

According to a very recent law, repetition is to be avoided till grade 9, and the schools can organize extra educational support for those having school difficulties. As we mentioned before, a Decree published in 1991 permits that handicapped children, recognized by the school authorities as such, can follow an 'alternative curriculum ' and be exempted from the common evaluation tests: in these cases, instead of a Diploma of Basic Education they are entitled to a Certificate of Basic School Attendance.

S. Pedro do Sul is a small town of 25,000 inhabitants, located in a rural area in the north-east of the country. The economy of this town relies essentially on agriculture, some small industries, and tourism which centres around the spa.

Until five years ago, this region was completely lacking in any kind of special educational resources. In 1989, a private association initiated an intervention which aimed to answer the various needs of the handicapped population and, with the collaboration of the Ministry of Education, a special education team was put into action. The policy of this association has been oriented towards the principles of integration and normalization, and regular pre-school facilities and schools have been encouraged to open their doors to children with different disabilities.

One of these schools is the local preparatory school, which initiated the integration of students with moderate learning difficulties during the school year of 1989/90. These students were considerably behind in their schooling: their basic academic skills were at the level of first or second grade. Nevertheless, they could all communicate verbally and had no motor problems. When these students were accepted into this school, the school principal and the resource teacher (specially appointed to work with them) agreed that their integration would be essentially social in nature, and that they could only attend regular classes in physical education and arts and crafts. Besides this, they were to participate with their non-disabled peers in all free-time activities, recreation, study visits and collective project work. The other academic subjects were to be taught by the resource teacher in a space specially designed for this purpose. For the majority of these students this meant reading, writing and arithmetic and some functional activities according to their individual needs.

After the first school year, this experiment was carefully evaluated by the school staff and the resource teacher and they concluded that the social integration of the students in question had succeeded, that they had improved their behaviour and that there was clear progress in their normalization. For their parents it was an obvious source of pride that their children could go to a regular school 'like all the others'. These positive results encouraged the teachers to take another step forward and to try the participation of these students in many other subjects, although with a different timetable in order to permit an individualized curriculum design. Some would stay longer in the special class; others would be oriented for a few hours a week to vocational training; while others would participate in almost all academic subjects in the regular class. This new approach provoked a greater participation amongst all teachers in this programme as they started to see these students as their own (like all the others) and to feel responsible for their school achievement. Simultaneously, the role of the resource teacher was reassessed, and a much closer link between the activities carried out in the regular and special classes was proposed.

During this last school year, the presence of these students was cause for a profound discussion among the school staff. 'We felt the need to rethink the intentions of the school and we realized that the school organization as it is cannot answer to the student's needs', the school director told me. The reform proposed by the school staff has the following main points.

First, there is a need to change the existing approach towards educational support given to students with school difficulties. The law permits that they receive extra academic support, in small groups, given by regular teachers. The experiment showed, however, that this approach was inefficient, as their learning problems were not solved by having more hours of teaching through the same methods. They have learning difficulties, mainly, because they find no meaning in school subjects, because they cannot cope with a series of 50-minute oral lectures, and because the rhythm of the teaching is not adapted to their own learning capacities. The teachers and the school principal realized that the new approach towards 'disabled' students was much more successful than the one used with the 'slow learners', as it permitted a more individualized programme, including different practical activities.

Second, there is a need to avoid the distinction between the two groups – those with mental disability and those having school difficulties – and to organize a global school strategy that could respond to each individual need. The strategy proposed entailed a profound change to the school system, based on separate subject teaching and the school staff is planning the following measures:

- Instead of having separate 50-minute classes for each subject, they will have long periods for different project-work activities involving different topics, coordinated between themselves and oriented by different subject teachers.
- The time-schedule established for students to attain the various levels of the curriculum will be adapted to each student.
- The resources available for the extra remedial classes will be used to complete the curriculum with activities related to arts, sports, computers, use of media, etc.
- This educational perspective will have the flexibility necessary to include all students, from the gifted to those with learning problems.

Here ends the brief description of these three schools. The Marinha Elementary School in Espinho, through the activity developed by a resource room, found a way to reach the needs of a severely socially and economically deprived population and was able to attract the students and their parents. The Anta Elementary School, in the same town, opened its doors to various children with severe disabilities and, in order to facilitate their participation in the school, broadened its methods and opened the school to the community. Finally, the preparatory school in S. Pedro do Sul, stimulated by the experimental integration of students with moderate learning problems, is implementing a profound change in the traditional teaching methods. The aim of all these schools is to be able to respond in the best way to the needs of all children in their community, whatever difficulties they may have.

As I said earlier, the selection of these schools was not based upon any systematic survey: they are examples chosen from many others that are following similar steps. We must say that we are very far from having, in Portugal, all schools as 'schools for all'. But we believe that the role played by those who are involved in this 'pioneer movement', in spite of all the existing negative conditions, will spread their influence in the near future.

Reference

Ainscow, M. (1991) 'Effective schools for all: an alternative approach to special education needs', in Ainscow, M. (ed.) *Effective Schools for All*, pp.I–19. London: David Fulton.

CHAPTER 9

The Emergence and Development of Integration in Spain

Carmen G. Pastor

Introduction

Special education has drastically changed in Spain during the last decade. This chapter tries to explain how integration has emerged and the most important ideas affecting its evolution up to today. Changing assumptions about the nature of special education has many implications for school organization and classroom practices and it often provokes conflicts between different individuals or interested groups. On this point, it is important to know the circumstances in which integration has emerged and the main groups interested in its development.

One of the circumstances that makes a difference between Spain and other European countries is that after the Second World War, many countries reorganized their educational systems and consolidated a special school system. Special education generates its own interests as an institutional system and, when integration began two decades ago, it had to deal with them. Tomlinson (1982) and Barton and Tomlinson (1984) have explained, from a sociological view, the implications of this situation, and Potts (1987) noted the two ways in which special education professionals may impede integration through patterns of work and power relationships. In this sense, the lack of a consolidated system of special education in Spain is an interesting advantage for developing integration, although it is important to notice that this 'advantageous' situation is associated with a poorly developed educational system (Pastor, 1993). The first part of this chapter concentrates in these factors.

The second part analyses the beginning of integration, regulations and the ideas developed, and the third part refers to problems in current integrational practice.

Antecedents

In Spain, we can not speak about integration separately from political change during the two last decades. In fact, the first reference for explaining the opportunity for a new legal frame is the Constitution promulgated in 1978, after a transitional term to the democratic system which began after Franco's death. Our 'Magna Carta' proposes democratic principles of social life and a new perspective to deal with the different conditions of people's lives, preventing discriminatory situations in two ways: a) through the development of public policies, and b) through a non-discriminatory educational system that has as its main aim to develop the human personality of individuals through democratic principles.

It is very important to note the meaning of this legal frame, because it was an opportunity for different social forces interested in people with handicaps who were working for improving their life conditions. These conditions were very poor up to the 1960s, and even after these years, in spite of several efforts, they did not improve too much. So this new political situation was considered an opportunity for social and political forces to work together.

In 1982, Social Integration of Handicapped People Act (*Ley de Integración Social de Minusvalidos*) was a result of this collaboration. The Act considered four issues:

- rehabilitation,
- assessment,
- education, and
- professional training.

In this way the Act tried to unify the different issues relating to people with handicaps and considered social integration as only one problem with different dimensions. Before the Act, each Department was working separately and coordinating efforts was the main problem for public services. Now the Act shared out different roles more equally for each service, but not the responsibility for social integration. In fact, the Act defined the concept of handicap as a result of social and environmental factors.

Inside this new legal framework, special education was considered as an integral, flexible and dynamic process that should be applied in an individualized way at each level of the educational system. The new aims of special education would be:

a) To overcome the conditions of handicap.
b) To learn the necessary knowledge and skills.
c) To develop individual ability and personality.
d) To integrate each individual into an adult life with autonomy through satisfactory conditions (job, culture, leisure, etc.)

Assessment of the child is considered the most important point for making a decision about the form of education, the placement of the child in the educational system and an individual programme. So it was also necessary to organize the assessment services in the educational system, which were previously poorly developed.

The new organization was an important precedent in the National Plan for Special Education which was being developed in an experimental way in designated areas of Spain from 1978. So the Act, in its educational issues, took its organizational basis from this Plan.

The first critical reflection on this point of the beginning of integration is that the Act considered special education on a basis which was formulated in very different circumstances, since, actually, in 1978 'integration' in Spain had a different meaning than in 1982. It is easy to understand the difference in the following definition of children who need special education:

> Special education is necessary, *sensu stricto*, by all children who during a significant step in their life cannot obtain advantages in ordinary school. In simple terminology, all these children will be called 'handicapped' (the original term in Spanish is '*deficientell*') – mentally, physically and sensorial handicapped people (*Plan Nacional de Educación Especial*, 1982, 77–8).

The Plan made a difference between children with handicaps and children with learning difficulties; it considered that the children with learning difficulties would have support services in their own school if possible. It sustains two different systems in education (ordinary and special) and only conceives of integration in pre-school level: 'At pre-school age the handicapped child should not stay separate from peers....The Ministry of Education ought to favour this integration' (*Plan Nacional de Educación Especial, 1982, 82*). In fact, they considered that integration is favoured if the percentage of special classrooms in ordinary schools grows and the percentage of special schools decreases (70 per cent of special classrooms and only 30 per cent in special schools is considered the correct proportion).

Although the principles of the Plan were integration and normalization, we must understand them with a restricted meaning. Another principle in the Plan was 'sectorization': this was an organizational principle which became very problematic, because it conceived special education services as being concerned with sectors of population. Under this organizational principle there was the concept of medical organization based on the pathological incidence of different handicaps (illness) in the population. In fact, the sector is conceived to include 250,000 or 300,000 inhabitants.

The Plan has two phases. The application of the first one implied:

- setting up multiprofessional teams,
- the sectorization of resources provision,
- setting up special classroom in ordinary schools, and
- experimental projects for special schools.

The second phase could not be developed because it coincided with a new organization of the Spanish State: some regions, like Catalonia, the Basque Country and others obtained autonomy and they would have their own planning for integration. However, the Plan was important as a basis for the first resource provision focused in multi-professional teams which had the following roles:

- detection,
- assessment and counselling, and
- early and pre-school intervention.

In spite of this critical view, the Plan reflects a great effort in 1978, because it was the first document in Spain on special education elaborated by experts. We can understand it as a challenge if we think that it was delayed from 1955, a year in which a mandate of the Ministry of Education ordered its formulation. Indeed, it is the first document in which the word 'integration' is expressed, even in this restrictive way. So the Act in 1982 had to take this one precedent.

Maybe it is necessary to have a look over political events again, and to note that in 1982 the general elections were won by the Socialist Party. In this way, it is easier to understand the future development of the Act, above all in education. So we must consider the development of integration at the same time as the development of new ideas in the educational system. The reform of the educational system had been a challenge, expressed finally in the 1990 Act of Education.

The real beginning of integration: the Royal Decree for Special Education Regulation (1985)

As I pointed out previously, the second phase of the National Plan for Special Education could not be applied, because each autonomous region assumed responsibility for organizing education. So, we have to consider two levels of political regulations: the national regulations for the whole Spanish State and the regulations, based on the national regulations, in the autonomous communities (regions).

For instance, Catalonia and the Basque Country started planning special education even before the 1982 Act. In Catalonia, a document dated 1981 defined special education as 'the whole of resources for each step in the ordinary educational system able to answer to the constitutional mandate'. They preferred to stress the concept of diversity rather than speaking about the integration of handicapped children in the school (Gine, 1986). In the Basque Country, a document dated 1982 noted the acceptance of individual differences, as one of the most important aims of education in Euskadi (*Departmento de Educación y Cultura del Pais Vasco*, 1982).

The Ministry of Education considered a national regulation was necessary for starting the integration process in the whole State, and in October 1982, they published a Royal Decree (RD). This document did not have an effective application and a new Royal Decree was published in 1985. This one was more directive in dealing with the start of the integrational process:

> ...the main lines of the present Royal Decree can be materialized, firstly, providing school institutions with the services which influence its functioning, favouring the educational process, avoiding segregation and facilitating integration for students with handicaps in school; secondly, the school institution has to consider the existence of special schools; and thirdly, it is necessary to set up a continuous coordination in the educational system, between ordinary and special schools (RD, 6 March 1985, Special Education Regulation).

The document give lines for actions, in fact it is the start of integration. The most important points in the 1985 RD are the regulations about, first, provision of services for supporting special education. The support includes three professional teams:

- a multiprofessional team for assessment,
- teachers support, and
- groups of therapists, mainly the language therapist, psychotherapist, physiotherapist and psychomotricist.

Second, there are regulations concerning curriculum adaptation for the practice of integration. The curriculum adaptation becomes a Programme for Individual Development (PDI) which has to be elaborated by support professionals.

Indeed, the RD requires from autonomous communities specific ways for implementing integration over an eight-year period (1986–1992).

During the three first years, the schools can ask the Educational Authorities for permission to become an integrated school, but later the Authorities required integration in schools where there was demand for it. It was very important at the beginning that the integrational principles and meanings were disseminated; then the Education Authorities participated in seminars and conferences explaining the new policies in education. The meaning of integration now included school improvement, the education policies were now trying to deal with a high percentage of failure in school:

> The integration project does not try only to promote integration for handicapped students previously allocated in special schools...but, at the same time, and with the same strength, to change the school, modifying educational conditions, providing support for many students who have difficulties in some level of their development. They must have a school with an organizational system able to provide resources, support, an adequate educational programme, everything possible to prevent the failure which is produced by a non-flexible school (Marchesi, 1986).

Eight points defined the new policies:

1. Early intervention is considered one of the most important issues for further integration.
2. Each primary school will progressively become an integrated school, changing ways for educating their students, with necessary support from the Educational Authorities.
3. Support teams will be increased.
4. Initial and In-service teacher training will deal with integration requirements.
5. A National Resource Centre will be set up for providing information, resources, training and research. It must be a point for reference, collection and initiative.
6. Special schools will be transformed with new resources.
7. It is necessary to change attitudes in school and society.
8. Teachers with motor and sensorial handicaps are able to teach as public servants.

The framework for intervention is similar, in terms of policy, to that of England; even educational authorities began to use the 'special educational needs' concept, because it included in integration this double process of inclusion for children with handicaps and no exclusion for children with difficulties in ordinary schools. The Warnock Report became an important reference and many experts from England came to Spain to explain the English experience in integration. This influence will be evident later, in the *White Book for Educational System Reform* (MEC, 1989), in which a chapter is dedicated to 'special educational needs':

> The main change is to include the concept of special educational needs. On the basis that all children need different individual support during the educational process for guaranteeing success in the goals of education, special educational needs refer to some children who, in a complementary way, need another kind of less usual support (p.163).

It is necessary to note that at the same time as the 1985 RD was published and integration began to develop, there was a debate in which ideas were quickly evolving. This evolution was not similar for the whole State, because each autonomous community had different circumstances which were defining the situation for dealing with integration as follows:

- social and economic differences,
- different school circumstances, previous integration, and
- different policies for solving educational problems.

If we have a look at these different communities we can see that some of them are very developed, like Catalonia or the Basque Country, although others are less developed, like Galicia or Andalusia. In the first cases, an important factor was the development of industry which had determined the social characteristics and had favoured a major demand for education. This demand had required an institutional answer and so, the most developed regions have set up the best conditions for improving their educational system. In this way, we found out that the more developed regions had an initial advantage for planning innovations in their schools. In fact, Catalonia and the Basque Country carried out the first regulations for integration. Indeed, there are other circumstances too, like the fact that each community had their own government, and so each had a way to solve their educational problems through their particular policies, which inevitably means that integration is conceived in different ways.

In fact, we can find out at the same time examples of 'inclusive education' and of 'the least restrictive environment' for students with handicaps. For instance, in Galicia, integration was resisted at the beginning: they preferred to set up new special classrooms in ordinary schools because they considered that integration was not proper and positive for some children with handicaps; they referred to this as a 'non-integration' (Perez Quintana, 1986, p.49) .

In Andalusia, the policy involved trying to lower the ratio of teacher/students in integrated classrooms, to convert special classrooms to resource classrooms and to increase support teachers in integrated schools; even children with severe forms of learning difficulties are integrated.

Present and future perspectives

Spain is at present a responsive country facing up to integration; although there are difficulties the common feeling is that integration is a path without return. The most important aim is now to consolidate the process, to prevent the possibility of stagnating.

The participants in the integration process consider as a condition *sine qua non* for improving it, that the provision of resources should increase. They argue that if resource provision does not increase, the integration process will stagnate. This argument is right if we think that in the present more and more children with special needs are been integrated into the ordinary school; but it could be inconclusive if it does not take seriously a more complicated problem referred to as 'profit-making' by schools and others involved in resource provision. Years ago, Birch and Reynolds (1982) noted a certain confusion about providing more and more resources and the need to reflect about it.

A study about integration in the province of Seville (Andalusia) found that 32 support teams for integration were created between 1986 and 1990. Each one had three professionals, and they have been collaborating with other teams which were previously working in the schools. But, the principals, classroom teachers and support teachers think that although many professionals go to their schools, they do not spend enough time to solve the educational problems. They do not want more professionals but more dedication, more involvement in the school life and its problems. Sometimes they ask for a specific professional to deal with individual needs. For instance, in some cases they consider it necessary to have a language therapist because in the school there are many children with language difficulties. Thus the problem is not only the increase of provision but the adequate meeting of real needs in each school (Pastor, 1993). The challenge now is to address this situation, and it is necessary to know in advance what are the needs which the real practice makes evident.

From a whole-school approach, where special needs are integrated in the common school needs, it is difficult to recognize who are the children who have to be included in an integration programme, if we consider educational needs as interactive, depending on the educational context (school organization and climate, curriculum, classroom practice, etc.). From the educational authorities' point of view, integration is a programme with a determined provision of resources, and even accepting a whole-school approach, they try to limit the consumers of this programme and to separate integration from other school needs. So, there are two antagonistic ways to understand integration. Sectorization as an organizational principle of integration is in opposition to the principles of the whole-school approach.

If integration processes call for more and more flexibility in adapting the programme to the characteristics of each school, then it is necessary that the educational authorities understand that it is an uncertain process which is difficult to plan outside each school. They need to collaborate and negotiate better, rather than give inadequate provision and wait for successful results.

Indeed, considering integration as a separate process from school becomes a source of conflict for relationships between involved and non-involved staff in schools. In fact, sometimes integration depends on determined individuals who have to bear too much responsibility, and that is not the best situation for consolidating integration. Mainly, integration has depended on teacher support: he/she has been responsible not only for each child with SEN but also for the whole organization of integration in each school. Many classroom teachers think that children with special needs must have a PDI; this programme is different to the classroom programme and, as a result, the children and the teacher must work independently all the time. In this sense the policy of the PDI has not favoured integration in classroom practice and classroom teachers' involvement. These difficulties are explained in the following paragraphs from support teachers interviews (Pastor, 1993):

> We try for students to have the opportunity to learn in the regular classroom, but we understand that this is very hard for classroom teachers (support teacher, case 10).

> I try doing integration in other ways and it is not possible because there is no collaboration from classroom teachers (support teacher, case 22).

Some support teachers also explain their relationships with support teams, pointing out that they organize the main work (Pastor, 1993):

> The external support team has to work in the school and, obviously, we accept

> this situation, but integration is our problem... anyway, we try to get co-ordination with them... (support teacher, case 3).

> Each support teacher has his/her children, the support team works directly with children or with the classroom teacher...but the support teacher organizes all the work...the support team works on 'special' problems (support teacher, case 4).

If the educational policy is to try to change the school, and integration is a part of this change, it will be necessary for the involvement of the whole school in making educational decisions for all the students. In an integrative school, not only students have educational needs but also school staff, as some authors have noted (Cunningham, 1982; Galloway, 1989; Lindsay, 1983). In Spain, classroom teachers say that they feel they are not ready for integration and they need training and assessing, as some research has concluded:

> Teachers seem to feel themselves let down during all the process or at some point of it. The lack of satisfaction is because they need support for implementing integration, through training for dealing with this new situation, through consulting... (Illan, 1989, p.132).

Spanish authors have considered proposals for meeting 'teachers special needs', but integration is also a problem of sharing responsibility. It is necessary to know the roles and functions for each member of school staff, including professionals who support integration. There is not only one model for integration: each school has to define its own model and evaluate it for improving or changing it.

In Spain, each school must elaborate an 'Educational Project'. This is a good opportunity for explaining what integration means in each case and how it is possible to translate into practice this particular means of integration. But sometimes 'Educational Project' and 'Integration Project' are different things for schools, because planning for action may be complicated for staff if they are not appropriately supported. Teachers Centres were created for developing and supporting educational initiatives, and they are potentially an important point of reference for the integration process. At the same time, the National Resources Centre for Special Education offers information, meetings and publications.

All seems ready in terms of the theory and planning for integration, but what is happening and what will be the future? The 1990 Act of Education (LOGSE) is positive because it has included integration in the educational system reform, but now headteachers, teachers, students, support teachers and support team members are worried because the Act is not detailed enough on many of the important issues. In fact, all is summarized in two points:

> Art. 35 – The educational system provides the necessary resources for students with temporary or permanent special needs; they can attain the same general aims in the same system established for all students.
>
> Art. 36 – For attaining the aims previously noted, schools must have the necessary organization, with teachers and specialized professionals, and resources for students who participate in the learning process. Indeed, it will be necessary to adapt and to diversify the curriculum for facilitating these aims.

These points do not introduce anything new and they are too imprecise. For instance, in Article 36.3. referring to the allocation in special classrooms or schools, they point out that students could be placed there when the ordinary school does not have adequate resources. The risk arises in knowing when adequate resources are or not available in the ordinary school and who decides. And in Article 36.3, referring to parents, their participation in educational decisions depends on further regulations by the Educational Authorities. The lack of compromise is evident and the fears increase when the economic situation is negative like it is at the moment.

The educational reform requires many resources and it is the main political focus for the Educational Authorities to consider that integration is already developed in the last years and now there is one system for all children. Nevertheless, the integration process needs to be reconsidered in respect to many issues. For instance, in the new levels of the educational system it can become problematic, especially in the new secondary education (12–16 years). In the past, primary education was up to 14 years, and many integrated children could receive an adapted/modified curriculum; now to pass from primary to secondary education may be a new risk (like it is in other countries). On the other hand, in the past, vocational training was possible between 14 and 18 years, and students with handicaps were integrated in vocational training schools. Now the question is whether secondary education will deal with the needs for training in vocational opportunities.

In spite of efforts made during the last decade, integration requires a careful answer to many questions about current practice in integrated schools. There is a tendency to consider education for all without assuming individual differences and needs. We must be ready to deal with the traditional and known policies in education, and it may be better to consider integration as a result of the process of education for diversity.

References

Barton, L. and Tomlinson, S. (1984) *Special Education and Social Interests.* Beckenham: Croom Helm.

Birch, J. W. and Reynolds, M.C. (1982) 'Special education as a profession'. *Exceptional Education Quarterly.* 2, 4, 1–13.

Cunningham, W.G. (1982) 'Teacher assistance teams: A model for within-building problem solving'. *Learning Disabilities Quarterly.* 2, 85–95.

Departamento de Educación y Cultura del Pais Vasco (Orden de 2 de Septiembre de 1982), *Euskal Herriko Hezkuntza Berezirako Egitamual (Plan de Educación Especial para el Pals Vasco,*. BO del Pais Vasco de 7 de Octubre.

Galloway, D. (1989) 'The special educational needs of teachers. In Barton, L. (ed) *Integration: Myth or Reality?* London: Falmer Press, pp.83–93.

Gine, C. (1986) 'La educacion especial y la integracion de los niflos disminuidos en Catalufial', Rodriguez, J.A. (coord.) *Intogración on ZGB: una nueva cocuela.,* Madrid: Fundacion Banco Exterior, pp.37–42.

Illan, N. (1989) La Integration Escolar y los Profesores, Valencia: Naus Llibres.

Lindsay, G. (1983) *Problems of Adolescence in Secondary School,* Beckenham, Croom Helm.

Marchesi, A. (1986) 'La situacion educativa del R.D. sobre la integracion escolar de niflos disminuidosl', in Rodriguez, J. A. (coord.) *Intagración an EGB: una nueva eocuola,* Madrid: Fundacion Banco Exterior, pp.31–6.

MEC (1989) '*Libro Blanco para la Reforaa del gistema Educativo,* Madrid: Ministerio de Educacion y Ciencia.

Pastor, C. (1993) 'Evaluating integration process', paper presented at 3rd Biennal Conference of IASE, Viena 5–9 July.

Plan Nacional de Educación Especial (1982) Madrid: Centro de Informacion sobre Deficiencias.

Perez Quintana, J.M. (1986) 'La integracion escolar en Galicial', in Rodriguez, J. A. (coord.): *Intagración an EGB: una nueva cocuela,* Madrid: Fundacion Banco Exterior, pp.49–57.

Potts, P. (1987) '*What difference would it make to the professionals?',* in Booth, T. and Potts, P. (eds) *Integrating Special Education,* Oxford: Blackwell.

Tomlinson, S. (1982) *A Sociology of Special Education.,* London: Routledge & Kegan Paul.

CHAPTER 10

Integration Practice and Policy in the UK for Pupils with Special Educational Needs

Christine O'Hanlon

Introduction

The United Kingdom is made up of England, Scotland, Wales and Northern Ireland. The education system as a whole in Britain applies to England and Wales; there are some minor differences in the law in Scotland and Northern Ireland. In the UK the principle that children with special educational needs (SEN) should be educated in ordinary schools is now part of education law. The 1981 Education Act was the government's response to the Warnock Report, published in 1978 after a five-year enquiry into special education in England and Wales. The new Act came into force on 1 April 1983. There are new duties for health authorities relating to children with (SEN) under the age of 5; if they think that a child may have SEN, they must inform the parent and bring it to the attention of the Local Education Authority (LEA in Britain) or Education Board (in Northern Ireland). The authority must also inform the parent of any voluntary organization relevant to the child's condition. The new legislation calls for radical new procedures for the identification, assessment and placement of children with SEN. Children with SEN cover a wide range of disability and include children referred to in European contexts as 'handicapped', a term which is now avoided in the UK because of its stigmatizing associations.

Children with SEN are now to be placed in ordinary schools, as long as certain conditions are met. The former categorization into different 'handicaps' has been abolished. The authorities must define the 'needs' of individual children and show how and where these needs will be met, rather than categorize the child and then place the child in a 'category' or school related to the handicap. Parents are now given much more information about their child. Consultations, discussions and the sharing of records and reports are of crucial importance in the 'statementing' or in the process of assessing children's needs. A 'statement' is an official document compiled as a result of a multi-disciplinary assessment of the child, which states the child's educational needs and the provision considered necessary by professionals to meet the child's needs in school or through extra support, help or therapy. The 'statement' is an official and legal entitlement to the fundamental help and support specified for the child in the document.

Essentially the new legislation in the UK ensures that:

- Categories of handicap are replaced by new ways of assessing and meeting children's special educational needs.
- Parents are generally encouraged to become more involved in the assessment of their child, and may influence the provision and placement of the child.
- Parents are guaranteed access to information about their child.
- Local Education Authorities (LEAs) and Boards must attempt as far as possible, as long as certain conditions are met, to educate children with SEN in ordinary schools.
- The 1981 Education Act recognizes that up to one in five children may have SEN at some time during their school career.

In Northern Ireland, similar legislation to the 1981 Education Act was established through the Education and Libraries Order (Northern Ireland) in 1986, which enshrines basically similar principles for children with SEN. It is difficult to define exactly what is occurring in the area of 'integration' or inclusive education in the UK when provision and services are undergoing major changes as a result of recent legislation. The most recent law in education has brought major changes to schools and has subsequently had an impact on children with SEN.

The Education Reform Act

The Education Reform Act (1988) has led to a significant curriculum reform in all schools through the establishment of a National Curriculum in state sector schools, which applies to all pupils aged 5–16 years.

However, the Education Reform Act does allow for some exceptions to the norm for those pupils unable to follow the full curriculum (usually pupils with statements of SEN) as follows:

1. Areas of the National Curriculum requirements may be lifted or modified in specified cases or circumstances, under regulations made by the Secretary of State. For example, where the National Curriculum requires certain kinds of practical work, alternative arrangements might be prescribed in the interests of safe working for those pupils with a physical disability.
2. Where a pupil with SEN is statemented under the 1981 Act, the special educational provision specified in the statement may allow for exclusion from, or modification of, the provisions of the National Curriculum if they are inappropriate for the pupil concerned.
3. Headteachers will be allowed to make temporary exemptions for individual pupils who are not statemented. The Secretary of State is empowered by the Act to make the necessary regulations and these will enable headteachers to decide for an individual pupil
   either that the National Curriculum shall not apply,
   or that the National Curriculum shall apply with specified modifications.
   The exemption or modification will apply for a maximum of six months in the first instance. It is hoped that at the end of that period the pupil might be able to return to an education which fully implements the requirements of the National Curriculum.
   Alternatively, the period might be used to decide that special educational provision for the pupil needs to be made under the terms of the 1981 Act.

General Provisions

The National Curriculum applies to county, voluntary, maintained special, and grant-maintained schools. The curriculum for a maintained school has to satisfy the requirements of the Act, which are that the curriculum should be; *balanced and broadly based* and *differentiated,* so that what is taught and how it is taught is matched to and develops individual pupils' abilities and aptitudes.

The National Curriculum Council (NCC) which is responsible for producing the actual curriculum documents, reassures parents, professionals and others concerned about the education of children with special needs with respect to their inclusion in curriculum plans. The NCC reaffirms the principle of *active participation* in the curriculum by the complete range of pupils with SEN (including those with profound and multiple learning difficulties), whether they are in special, primary, middle or secondary schools, with or without statements.

They are aware of the very diverse range of pupils with SEN and do

They are aware of the very diverse range of pupils with SEN and do not underestimate the task of achieving greater participation in mainstream educational contexts. The NCC, in consultation with interested parties, revealed the need for nonstatutory guidance on increased participation in schools. The Council is also responsible for producing detailed guidance and advice for schools which are considering the inclusion of pupils with SEN. The NCC states:

> that participation in the National Curriculum by pupils with SEN is most likely to be achieved by encouraging good practice for all pupils. Special educational needs are not just a reflection of pupils' inherent difficulties or disabilities; they are often related to factors within schools which can prevent or exacerbate some problems. For example, schools that successfully meet the demands of a diverse range of individual needs through agreed policies on teaching and learning approaches are invariably effective in meeting special educational needs. It follows from this that pupils with SEN should not be seen as a fixed group; their needs will vary over time and in response to school policies and teaching. Liaison between special and primary and secondary schools fostered through implementing the National Curriculum and the planned involvement of INSET (in-Service courses) of all teachers of pupils with SEN, including LEA SEN support staff, will be important in achieving access to the National Curriculum for all pupils.' (NCC, 1989, para.5).

'INSET' is the acronym used for the in-service education of teachers, and is an area where provision of services is presently being undertaken by LEAs and Boards as well as, and often in partnership with, higher education institutions. The financing of INSET in support of developing the expertise of mainstream teachers in the integration of pupils with SEN is often viewed as an additional burden on LEA budgets, as there is often a requirement for extra and much-needed educational support to be brought and bought in to meet pupils' special educational needs.

Assessment and Local Management

To ensure that pupils with SEN would have equal opportunity to the school curriculum, a Code of Practice has been published giving practical guidance to LEAs and the governing bodies of all maintained schools on their responsibilities towards all children with SEN. It has been estimated that nationally, some 20 per cent of the school population will have special educational needs at some time in their school career. The Code of Practice concerns the identification and assessment of pupils with SEN and came into effect on 1 September 1994. The Code places responsibilities on LEAs and schools, the health services and social

- all children with SEN should be identified and assessed as early as possible;
- provision for all children with SEN should be made in the school in partnership with the child's parents; no statutory assessment is necessary;
- there must be close cooperation between all the agencies concerned and a multi-disciplinary approach to the resolution of issues.

The Code recommends a five-stage model in recognizing the special educational needs of pupils, as follows:

1. The Class or subject teacher identifies the child's special educational needs and, in consultation with the school's SEN coordinator, takes initial action.
2. The SEN coordinator takes a lead in gathering information and for coordinating the child's special educational provision, working with the child's teachers.
3. Teachers and the SEN coordinator are supported by specialists from outside the school.
4. The LEA considers the need for a statutory assessment and, if appropriate makes a multi-disciplinary assessment.
5. The LEA considers the need for a 'statement' of SEN and, if appropriate, makes a 'statement' and arranges, monitors and reviews provision.

The Code was necessary for a number of reasons: to ensure the effective meeting of children's SEN in mainstream schools by matching practice and provision to need; the creation of individual education plans and the involvement of outside specialists; the requirement for LEAs to observe the new regulations, including the statutory time limits. The implementation of the Code is being closely monitored and may be revised in the future in light of the results. However, it is generally welcomed by professionals as an improvement because it sets out stages and responsibilities for professionals to find the best provision for pupils with SEN.

The situation is ambiguous in relation to supporting the access of all children to the National Curriculum because of its associated assessment at age 7, 11, 14 and 16 years. Pupils in special education have freedom of choice to study what they like or what the school offers, with optional assessment and examinations, whereas pupils included in the National Curriculum are subjected to regular assessment through a series of Standard Assessment Tasks (SATs) which measures their level of attainment. This puts pressure on both the teachers and pupils to meet specific nationally defined attainment criteria. However, adhering to the National Curriculum is generally held to be an issue of 'inclusion' in mainstream education, and it is seen to bring more children in special schools up to mainstream standards, through exposure to a wider, more balanced, relevant and differentiated curriculum. The Task Group on Assessment and Testing (TGAT, DES, 1988) acknowledged the value of NC attainment targets for SEN pupils. They state:

> ...like all children, those with SEN require attainable targets to encourage their development and promote their self-esteem. We therefore recommend that wherever children with SEN are capable of undertaking national tests, they should be encouraged to do so.

Another factor which is influencing the progress of inclusion in education at present is the Local Management of Schools (LMS). The 1988 Act required every LEA or Board to prepare a scheme for the local management of schools. Under LMS schemes, local authorities have discretion as to whether or not they delegate provision for pupils with statements of SEN in ordinary schools and special units organized as part of ordinary schools. Where such provision is delegated, the formula for allocating resources to schools must take account of the need to channel resources to meet the particular needs of pupils in such schools. The local authority will retain its duty under the 1981 Act to ensure that the special educational provision specified in the statement is made for pupils with statements, and will be expected to reflect this in the conditions of the scheme. It will be for the school to consider how best to deploy its overall resources in order to offer the necessary provision, but it will also be obliged to offer what is specified in the statement.

LMS is the delegation of the management of a school to its local managers, which normally comprises the headteacher and the governing body. LMS has been introduced progressively since April 1990 to all government controlled schools, and has resulted in more schools having a greater say in decisions relating to resource allocation. This has led to schools looking at their own priorities for making decisions about what will be funded and reviewing their changing demands on resources. Pupils with SEN do not always benefit from the new arrangements and there are marked differences in the allocation of resources in schools, as there is no specified budget laid down by the government or the local authority.

The most crucial area for decisionmaking is that of staffing in the school. The number of staff and the balance of expertise within the school must be considered, e.g. teaching staff, nonteaching staff and additional staff for children with SEN, both with or without statements. There is also the consideration of the financial cost of in-service training to develop the expertise of the existing school staff, and the cost of books and other materials, equipment including Information Technology (IT), and library provision.

When LMS was first mooted for schools there was concern raised for pupils with SEN. A senior SEN adviser based in Knowsley wrote to the *Times Educational Supplement* to voice his concern about LMS, which he believes,

> poses much more of a threat to the integration process than any previous legislation. There is evidence of increased and increasing demand for segregated provision in many authorities. The problem is not unique to Knowsley (P. Horn, *TES*, 17 May 1991).

Segregated provision has increased in this local authority by 24 per cent. The fact that schools can now use open enrolment and that schools' examination results are to be published, is encouraging schools to compete with each other for better examination results, and makes them reluctant to enrol pupils with SEN who may not enhance the 'league tables'. This applies particularly to the large number of pupils with learning difficulties, with or without statements of SEN.

Local authorities now organize their own budgets and this offers some protection to statemented pupils, as they are legally ensured of funds. Yet there is also evidence of an increase in the numbers of 'statements' being prepared for pupils, as schools try to ensure money to meet the extra provisions required for children with SEN to be educated in the mainstream. Because of this situation, it is difficult to make definitive progress or to implement any new policies for greater inclusion in mainstream education, even where the political will exists.

Variation in Provision

There is great disparity between local authorities in the UK in their prioritizing of educational funding and their support of inclusion/integration. The Centre for Studies on Inclusive Education (CSIE) has recently presented an analysis of the statistics on segregation and inclusion in English LEAs (Norwich, 1994). A summary of the main conclusions drawn from the study are:

- in 1991/92 there was a small increase in special school placements;
- in 1992 the special school population overall went up from 1.47 per cent to 1.49 per cent of all 5–15-year-old pupils;

- there are wide variations in placements for pupils with SEN in different LEAs throughout the country;
- the highest segregating authority has 2.98 per cent of pupils in special schools, classes or units;
- the lowest segregating authority places 0.45 per cent of pupils in special schools, classes or units.

However, in relation to mainstream schools, it was found that:

- 42 per cent of all pupils with SEN statements were in mainstream schools – 32 per cent in ordinary classes and 10 per cent in special classes;
- one local authority placed 83.7 per cent of children with SEN statements in ordinary/mainstream schools;
- another local authority placed 11.3 per cent of children with SEN statements in ordinary/mainstream schools;
- 58 per cent of pupils with statements in England are educated in special schools.

The 'integration' of pupils is the common term used in European contexts, yet it covers a range of meanings from simple locational to social and functional integration as outlined in the Warnock Report (1978), to a range of more complex definitions of the process. Integration is generally agreed to be a 'process' of planned and continuous interaction with peers in an education setting. Hegarty (1993) points out that integration and segregation are not mutually exclusive concepts. Some forms of integration may overlap with what is viewed as segregation and both may coexist within a single school in various forms. The UK system is difficult to critique because although there are facts and figures like those produced by CSIE (Norwich, 1994), one cannot make qualitative comparisons of different forms of integration because of the local variations of practice within different LEAs in England, and also between Scotland, Wales and Northern Ireland. However, Cornwall consistently has the distinction of being the LEA with the highest percentage of children with 'statements' in ordinary schools and it is also one of the two LEAs with the lowest number of pupils in special schools.

Integration or inclusive provision for pupils with SEN is met through a range of organizational placements, e.g. special school, special school links with ordinary schools, units within or on the campus of mainstream schools and ordinary schools. There is also part-time placement, withdrawal systems and in-class support. Increasingly there is concern about the quality of the education received by pupils in ordinary school placement where 'inclusion' is the overriding aim. In England, Cornwall LEA is the authority with the lowest number of pupils in special schools; it is teacher attitudes to pupils in Cornwall, with its small scattered population, which are seen to be a key factor in successful inclusion practices (Portwood, 1994).

The willingness and competence of teachers to adapt the curriculum to allow access to pupils with SEN is central to their successful inclusion in ordinary schools (Slee, 1993). So too are class size, appropriate facilities and well-designed and adapted buildings. The Audit Commission (1992) reports that many LEAs are increasingly developing resourced schools for groups of children with similar learning needs to ensure qualitative provision.

There is a debate now about the benefits and effectiveness of link-schemes between ordinary and special schools. Mostly these schemes operate through 'bussing' pupils from special to ordinary schools. Whether this travelling brings any benefit to pupils is questionable; however, Jowett *et al.* (1988) see the links as a step to further placement, access to a broader curriculum and wider social contacts. They point out that this system makes great demands on pupils in terms of adaptation to a new school organization, system and social context. There is agreement generally about the need for a careful choice in school placements (Hegarty, 1993; Howarth, 1987) in insuring positive attitudes to the inclusion of pupils on the part of headteachers, staff and school governors. There is also a need to select children who can cope with the social demands of 'inclusion' when considering school placement.

Lorenz (1995) reports that one particular LEA provided both the required funding to enable children to be supported in their local school and the training needed to change the expectations of those involved in assessment and teaching. She found that once mainstream placement was seen as the norm rather than the exception, the inclusion of pupils with SEN became largely self-perpetuating.

A workshop held by CSIE in 1992 considered the vision of an inclusive UK education system in which the needs of all children, disabled and non-disabled, are to be met in schools and colleges. The key issues to emerge were that:

- achieving an inclusive education service is part of the human rights struggle against discrimination;
- inclusion has to be total if it is to work;
- disabled people who have been through the segregated system should be involved in planning and implementing the new inclusive system;

- there is no separate category of teaching skills for children with disabilities or difficulties in learning.

Conclusion

There is a complexity of provision in the UK, with evidence of much good practice but little uniformity from LEA to LEA, and no direct policy from the Department for Education in London.

In many ways certain projects for including pupils in mainstream education are an example to everyone of what can be achieved where there is a will and a vision, and when the quality of the child's or young person's educational experiences are put to the fore. An example of such a resolute aim is shown by Bishopswood Special School in Oxfordshire, which has succeeded in integrating/including half of its pupils with physical and mental handicaps into nearby mainstream schools. In 1981 the school transferred seven children and their teacher and helper from the special school to an empty classroom in the local primary school. The original seven children were selected because they could walk, were reasonably toilet-trained, could sit with some help and could feed themselves. The transferal was so successful that in 1982 another eight children were transferred, again with their teacher and classroom assistant. On this occasion however, the children were not carefully selected and included a child with autism and others who had little speech and were not toilet-trained. The LEA backed the transfers and spent £3,000 on sluices, washing machines, dryers and ramps. The room where the children spend most of the time is right at the centre of the school and therefore provides good opportunities for children throughout the school to interact together. When 200 parents of the 'ordinary' pupils were asked if they thought integration was a good thing, 91 per cent answered 'Yes' (Orton, 1985).

The school proved to many sceptics that children with severe learning difficulties could be successfully integrated into mainstream, with benefits to all the children concerned and not just the children with SEN.

The 1981 Education Act provided the framework for action for LEAs to develop their 'inclusion' practices in schools. It now appears that the legislation was not sufficient to ensure its efficiency or efficacy. Levels of LEA funding designated for pupils' needs, directly related to 'inclusion' and its effective resourcing, vary enormously and are locally set and administered. The commitment to inclusive education involving identifiable local budgets for the purpose, providing guidelines for schools and increasing the necessary training and support for teachers, are all areas that require further and better attention from policy makers and practitioners. There is an opportunity for all those concerned with the education of pupils with SEN – children, parents and professionals – to coordinate their demands and energies towards the realization of better practice based on the improved quality of provision. In spite of legislation, only the individuals involved with particular pupils can make this happen. With schools' preoccupation with meeting the requirements of the National Curriculum and trying to ensure that pupils score well on the new compulsory testing arrangements, meeting pupils' special needs will be a low priority. This, coupled with provisions in the 1988 Act which allow children with special needs to be excluded from all or part of the National Curriculum, may lead to more segregation within ordinary schools and a tendency to try to 'de-select' more pupils for segregated special education.

References

Audit Commission (1992) *Getting in on the Act*, London, HMSO.

CSIE (1992) *The Integration Charter Conference Report*, London, Centre for Studies on Inclusive Education.

DES (1988) *National Curriculum: Task Group on Assessment and Testing,* London: HMSO.

Hegarty, S. (1993) 'Reviewing the Literature on Integration', *European Journal of Special Educational Needs,* 8, 3.

Howarth, S. (1987) *Effective Integration,* Windsor, NFER-Nelson.

Jowett, S. Hegarty, S. and Moses, D. (1988) *Joining Forces,* Windsor, NFER-Nelson.

Lorenz, S. (1995) 'The placement of pupils with Down's Syndrome: a survey of one northern LEA', *British Journal of Special Education*, 22, 1.

NCC (1989) *Circular No. 5*, York: National Curriculum Council.

Norwich, B. (1994) *Segregation and Inclusion: English LEA Statistics 1988–92,* London: CSIE.

Orton, C. (1985) 'Integration'; in *Education the way forward*', London CSIE.

Portwood, P. (1994) *An Experience of Integration,* London: Children Nationwide.

Slee, R. (1993) 'Inclusive learning initiatives: educational policy lessons from the field', in Slee, R. (ed.) *Is There a Desk with My Name on it? The Politics of Integration*, London, Falmer Press.

CHAPTER 11

A Case Study. Integration through Cooperation: Returning Pupils to Mainstream School

A. Dens and E. Hoedemaekers

Introduction

In Belgium, children with serious learning difficulties attend a special school. If the regular/mainstream school is unable to cope with the children's problems, the authorities tend to assume that these pupils can return to a mainstream school, if they are provided with the extra facilities offered by the special school system. However, the expectation of returning to a mainstream school is rarely fulfilled, as the possibility of returning is a direct condition of the initial acceptance of the child in the special class.

At the Parkschool, a type-8 special school (for pupils with serious learning difficulties; see O'Hanlon, 1993) organized by the municipality of Leuven, this problem was identified a long time ago. It was found that most new pupils were at least 9 years old, and presented a grade level retardation of two to three years. That meant that the teaching objective for pupils in a type-8 school, i.e. the reintegration of pupils into mainstream education, was nearly impossible to achieve. Once this fact was recorded, the idea of aiming for an early but temporary placement for pupils identified with learning difficulties took hold. The result was that a play-learning class (or transition class) was set up in special schools with the aim of catering for 6-year-olds who, as a result of serious interruption or delay in their development, are in great danger of failing their first year in mainstream school.

Together with the pupils involved, a programme focusing on learning conditions and attitudes was completed with the view of readmitting them, after one year to the first year of mainstream education. The prospective 'return' is put forward as the central aim from the outset.

To make the system work, the cooperation of special education with mainstream education has to be set in motion by involving the guidance services in the successive stages of the project. Cooperation really gets off the ground when new pupils arrive at the special school and later, when their progress is being assessed. As a pupil changes over to a mainstream school, exhaustive consultations take place. Both teams have their part to play in the follow-up of the pupil's first year in mainstream education.

Parents take a central position in the whole process: they are kept informed all along the line, they can have their say at every step, so that in the end they can take the necessary decisions about their children by themselves.

This integration project has yielded satisfactory results. Data collected over the last six years prove that more than 50 per cent of 6-year-olds are able to return to mainstream primary education after one year in special education. Moreover, a follow-up study shows that in 95 per cent, of cases this kind of educational guidance is a success.

Cooperation of the two education systems also means that staff members have the opportunity of getting to know each other's working methods and that the school guidance services obtain more correct data, thus enabling them to give the help required. This kind of cooperation also ensures that special education staff can give more adequate support and invest more time and effort in the transition from a special to a mainstream school.

One of the recommendationsof this project is that every effort should be made to ensure that the two kinds of school cooperate. Their cooperation could well result in the gradual introduction in mainstream schools of those elements of special education that are particularly strong and beneficial to pupils.

Furthermore, measures should be taken in the area of educational guidance. The quality of the individual teacher is of the utmost importance here. In mainstream as in special education it is advisable to invest more than is the case at present in the training and support of teachers, as they are key figures in both special and mainstream education.

Learning difficulties in pre-school and primary education

Data resulting from a survey of pupils with serious learning difficulties in the Flemish primary schools show that a large number of pupils are lagging behind at school or have dropped out from the start. Van Damme (1992) has studied a cohort of pupils and concluded that 18.3 per cent of pupils in the 6th grade of the primary school show retardation. His analysis demonstrates that grade level retardation is a frequent phenomenon at given moments in a pupil's school career. Some 3 per cent of pupils already lag behind at the start of the first year of the primary school. Half the cases of delay in school subjects are recorded during that first year.

Thys and Van De Ven (1985) have tried to define this group of problem pupils. They found that 25 per cent of pupils in primary education are experiencing learning difficulties. Just over half of the pupils in this group have additional problems, i.e. their attitude towards work and/or their social interaction. These figures speak for themselves. A great number of pupils face educational problems at an early age despite the favourable teacher/pupil ratio in ordinary/mainstream pre-school and primary education.

In recent years, a number of policies have been adopted in order to prevent failure at school, for instance by setting up remedial classes (1974) and by the introduction of a specific teaching time allocation (1984). The remedial class is meant for primary school children whose educational achievement is low. In 1974 it was decided that the larger mainstream schools could set up a remedial class. A remedial teacher could be appointed as an extra member of the teaching staff. The task of the remedial teacher consists in organizing remedial activities for children of normal ability, who are experiencing mild learning difficulties, or to help pupils who have to catch up due to unforeseen circumstances.

In the statutory rules, no provision is made for the appointment of remedial teachers in smaller schools (less than 292 pupils), despite the fact that some schools amalgamated in order to comply with the official norm, which resulted in 20 per cent of pupils who cannot attend a remedial class.

With the introduction of the teaching time allocation in 1984, a solution to the problem of helping pupils with mild learning difficulties was in sight. From that moment on schools could decide independently how to share out the prescribed teaching load among all staff members. This measure was taken in the context of a general policy aiming at deregulation and promoting the autonomy of the individual school. The authorities fully expected that all schools would welcome the opportunity to schedule a post for a remedial teacher, to support and to organize the required amount of remedial activities necessary in the schools.

Three years later, it was found that this policy had some unwanted side-effects. A large number of schools had opted for educational convenience, namely small classes with a lower number of pupils, instead of arranging for a specialist teacher to be appointed in a remedial post. Since then, only 60 per cent of pupils can call on the help of a remedial teacher. Despite the good intentions displayed by the authorities, the expected results did not materialize. We have learned since that the remedial classes organized in mainstream education are gradually decreasing in number. Moreover, there is a marked increase in therapies being applied outside the school and in the special school type-8 classes (Ruijssenaars and Counet, 1991).

Learning difficulties in special education

Special education got its permanent structure when the 1970 Act was passed. The Act outlined eight types of special education, each of which has its own objectives, contents, methods and organization. All special schools acquired an autonomous status and were organized as separate entities, totally unconnected with mainstream education.

A type-8 school is adapted to the educational needs of children and young people with serious learning difficulties, which cannot be explained away by mental deficiency. In Flanders, type-8 classes take up more or less 30 per cent of the total number of pupils in special primary education. Type-8 classes are organized only at primary level with the aim of teaching the primary curriculum to pupils with special educational needs. Type-8 schools prepare pupils for reintegration into a mainstream school, in a primary class or, at the latest, during the transition from primary to secondary education.

Since 1986 the number of type-8 pupils has grown considerably, mainly due to a combination of two factors. In 1986 the clause blocking the development of special education since 1973 was abolished as a matter of policy, so that type-8 schools could be set up or remodelled. There has also been a noticeable change in the activities of the school guidance services (PMS), as a result of which more attention is now being paid to pre-school and primary education.

As far as type-8 orientation is concerned, we find that many newly arrived pupils are generally arriving late to special education and show serious learning difficulties, sometimes presenting two to three years' grade level retardation. However, research has shown that learning difficulties are detected early on (in more than 90 per cent of cases before the end of the first primary school year), but that referral to a type-8 school can take time, so that existing problems grow more complex during the delay in transfer to a special school.

Model Unit 'Parkschool'

The municipal school for type-8 special education, Parkschool, in Leuven has a clearly defined aim which is the reintegration of pupils into mainstream education. For this specific purpose a play-learning class was set up in order to provide the early but temporary placement of pupils in a type-8 special class.

The Parkschool evolved from classes for pupils with special educational needs, which originally were part of a mainstream primary school-cum-pre-school classes, and became a separate entity in 1973, some years after the 1970 Act had made the provision that all special classes organized in a mainstream school should be transformed into an independent special school.

From when it was first set up, the school saw a steady increase in its population; at the same time the chronological age of the newly arrived pupils dropped. Now it is markedly lower than the average age of pupils in other, similar schools elsewhere in Flanders (see Figure 11.1).

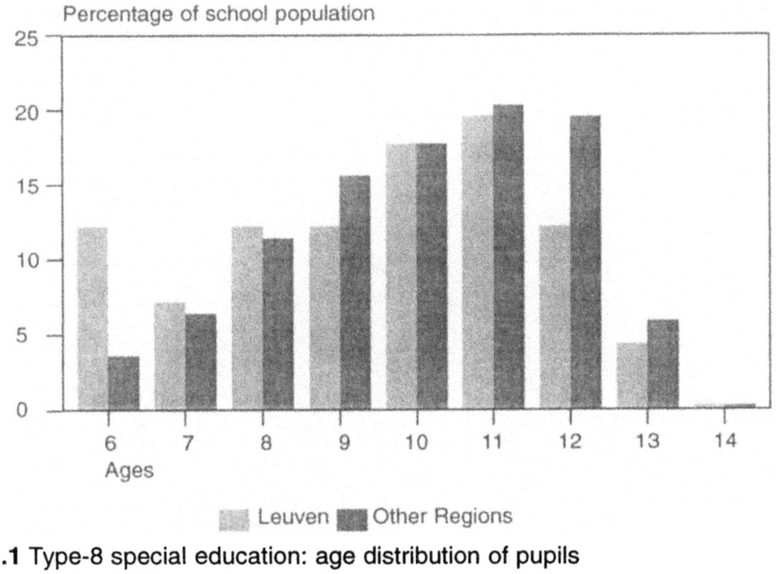

Figure 11.1 Type-8 special education: age distribution of pupils

As far as the inflow of new pupils is concerned, we can see that on average they tend to get younger every year. The number of 6-year-olds is on the increase, the number of 7- and 8-year-olds remains stable and the number of pupils who are 11 or over is decreasing (see Figure 11.2).

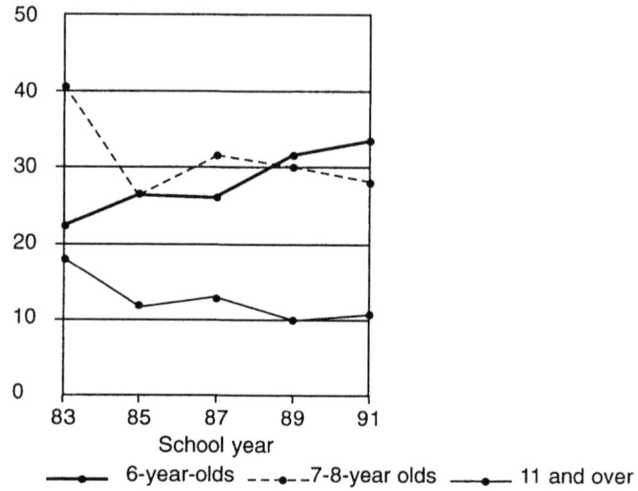

Figure 11.2 Parkschool: evolution of the inflow, 1983–91

We further notice that the outflow figures indicate a steady evolution. A growing number of 7-year-olds have left the school already, while the number of 10-year-olds remains stable and the number of 13-year-olds decreases (see Figure 11.3).

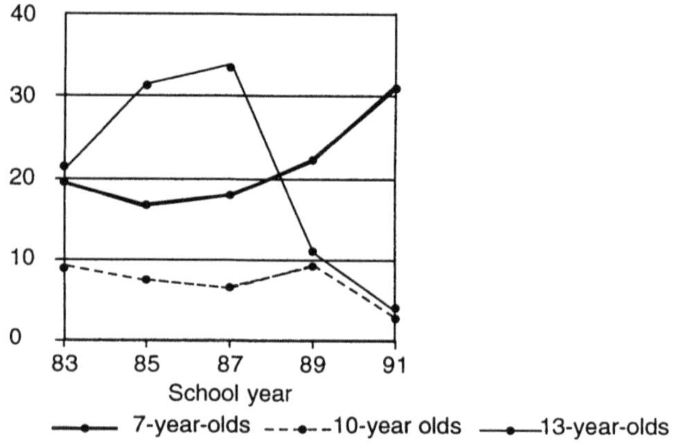

Figure 11.3 Parkschool: the outflow, 1983–91

For the school year 1991–92, stratified sampling of the parents' status reveals that 6 per cent of the pupils have at least one parent whose professional status implies that he/she has a university degree. In 37 per cent of cases, at least one parent has either further educational qualifications, or an upper-secondary level certificate; 39 per cent of pupils have at least one parent whose occupation implies that he/she has a lower-level secondary certificate or vocational secondary level qualifications. Eleven per cent of pupils have at least one parent who is an unskilled worker.

Parallel to the increase in the number of pupils, we see an increase in staff members. Since the teaching time allocation system was introduced in 1984, a relatively large number of periods are kept free for some specialist teachers, so that they can give individual lessons and organize extra educational activities in or outside classrooms. Only half the available hours go to the class teachers; the other half is shared out equally between the paramedical staff and the specialist teachers.

Organization

The above data on staff tell us something about the way the school is run. If we take the optimum use of the allocated resources as a central starting point, then we should apply them to break through the rigid class grouping system.

The school operates at four levels; every level encompasses a unit of work offering various opportunities for differential treatment of the individual pupils. The level of the *play-learning group* is meant for 6-year-olds with serious developmental deficiencies, who are unable to cope in the first primary year (see below). At the *initial level,* elementary arithmetic and reading are taught in various pedagogical units, depending on the subject matter already absorbed. At the *advanced level*, the initial knowledge and skills acquired and developed earlier on are more firmly structured and fixed in the pupil's memory. In the *upper level* classes, the minimum curriculum of primary education is studied.

The school has another special feature. Its expert teachers take up a large part of the teaching time budget (one quarter of the total allocation). They are responsible for any support given individual pupils and devote half their time to supportive action meant to sustain the instructional process. They devote the other half of their teaching time to support work for their colleagues in the classroom.

Consultations are expressly scheduled to take place at meetings of the class board, where staff members assess the pupils' performance and development. Special emphasis is laid on the need for transferable information.

The play-learning class

Soon after the school was set up, it was noticed that the majority of new pupils were children of 9 and over, with two or three years' grade level retardation. They arrived too late for the school to achieve its objective in time, namely the reintegration of these pupils in mainstream education while still of primary school age.

That is why a play-learning class was organized with clear and sound objectives: to offer pupil with learning disabilities an *early* special reception, but on a *temporary* basis, and with a *complementary* character to mainstream education. Activities in the play-learning class are expressly geared to the early return of children to the local mainstream primary school.

The pupils

The play-learning class is intended for 6-year-olds who are at great risk of failing their first year in a mainstream school due to grave lacunae in their cognitive development, without being mentally retarded.

More than half (59 per cent) of the pupils have an intelligence quotient which is higher than 90 (see Figure 11.4).

As to the pupils' social background, it appears that, compared to the total type-8 school population, four times as many pupils come from a social environment where at least one parent has an occupation requiring a university-type education.

How it works

The play-learning class is above all meant to bring about reintegration into ordinary education. Each return serves the purpose of narrowing the gap between mainstream and special education.

That objective is attained by working on the learning conditions and the learning attitudes via an adaptive programme based on task evaluation (which determines the approach used). In this way an effort is made to prepare the pupils for arithmetic and language lessons, all the

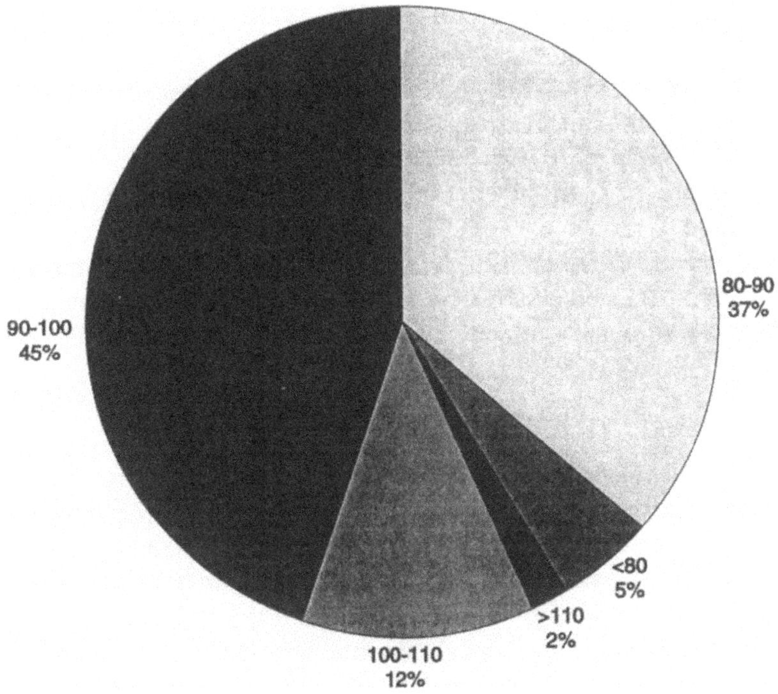

Figure 11.4: Intelligence: pupils of the play-learning class

while building up motivation, concentration and goal-oriented behaviour, as these qualities are often lacking. Motor development, particularly fine motor development, gets special attention. In class, the speech therapist works at stimulating the pupils' language development and vocabulary growth. If necessary, he/she provides the adequate individual therapy sessions. Language development and practising elementary arithmetic are encouraged all along. Social and personality development are also priority subjects.

From the child's reception in the play-learning group onwards, parents are closely involved. They are present at the discussions that are scheduled to take place at the beginning and at the end of the school year. They are highly valued as partners during consultations and planning sessions. As they are the persons ultimately responsible for the child's welfare, they should be able to make the necessary decisions by themselves.

Re-orientation

Intake procedure

When a pupil is referred to this special school class, the mainstream school, together with the school's guidance centre, are truly involved. This is the best way to collect useful first-hand information, so that the expectations of both teacher and parents can be anticipated and harmonized.

The duration of the child's planned stay in special education is agreed on, as the return to mainstream education is a built-in component of the intake procedure and is always borne in mind.

Preparation for the pupil's return

As soon as the period agreed on is over, all parties involved are asked to assess the pupil's chances of a successful return to mainstream education. An inventory of the chances and the remaining needs is made, after which the search for a mainstream school is on. This school should be able to receive the pupil under optimum conditions. Plans for the pupil's return are negotiated with the school, in order to reach agreement on the problems to be tackled, the cooperation to be arranged, and the period when assessment will take place.

Follow-up

At the beginning of the school year, an introductory talk is scheduled in order to present the pupil whose return is imminent. On this occasion the class teacher, the (PMS) counsellor and the parents are present. The 'returned' pupil's progress is followed up throughout the year. In the meantime, the parties concerned remain in contact over the phone. If a problem arises, another consultation is laid on. An assessment interview is scheduled for the end of the school year.

Parents

What strikes one most is that the parents are placed in a central position, as they are involved by right in each phase of the procedure. After all, it is the parents' task to come to the right decision about the choice of a school.

Evolution

Data collected over the last seven years show that more than 50 per cent of pupils in the play-learning class are able to return to a mainstream school (see Figure 11.5). It seems there is a connection between intelligence and the chances of returning to a mainstream primary school. The higher the pupil's intelligence level, the greater his/her chances of returning to an ordinary school (see Figure 11.6).

A follow-up study of 102 pupils over a period of six years shows that this orientation is successful in 95 per cent of cases. Figure 11.7 demonstrates that the number of pupils who return to ordinary primary education has diminished slightly over those six years, a fact that should not surprise anyone, as a number of children at risk are advised, on their return to a mainstream school, that they can always come back to the special school if anything goes wrong.

Evaluation

Orientation to special education

Although serious learning difficulties usually are diagnosed in time (in 65 per cent of cases before pupils start primary education, in 90 per cent of cases before they have completed the first primary year), it appears that referral to type-8 education is not advised until later on.

Thirty per cent of pupils are referred after two years in primary education, 40 per cent are referred after three years in primary education. In two-thirds of cases, the advice concerning referral to special education is given by the PMS-guidance centre. In other cases, advice is sought from other guidance services. Some parents seek advice on their own initiative. Two-thirds of parents follow that advice without delay. Other parents decide to take the step later on, or not at all.

This delay is caused by several factors. One is the segregation which is engendered by special education and the mistaken image it creates in people's minds. Moreover, it seems that the PMS-centre's advice sometimes clashes with the teacher's opinion given to the parents. Or, the parents lack insight into the complex problems their child has to face. The decisive factors here are of the same nature.

On the one hand, more substantial information about type-8 education should be made available in order to counteract any prejudice parents might have against special education, while on the other hand, the aggravation of the difficulties, together with a better understanding of the problems they engender, should prompt the parents to take the crucial step.

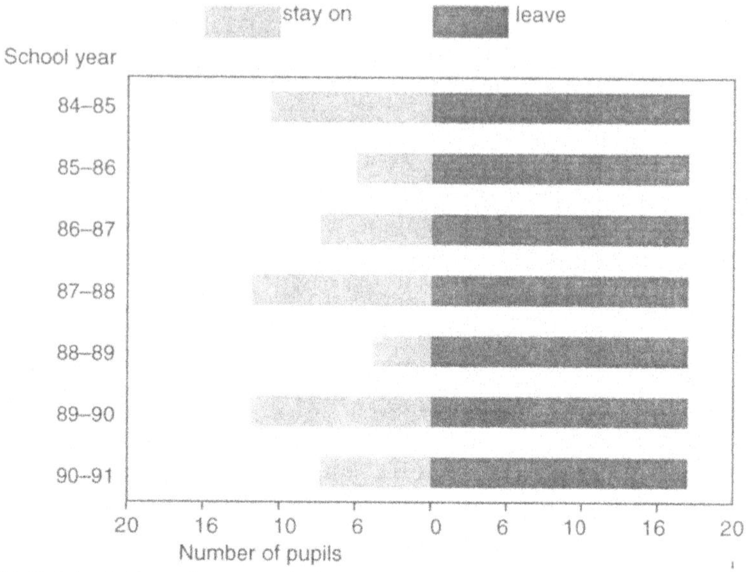

Figure 11.5 Orientation after completion of the play-learning class, 1984–91

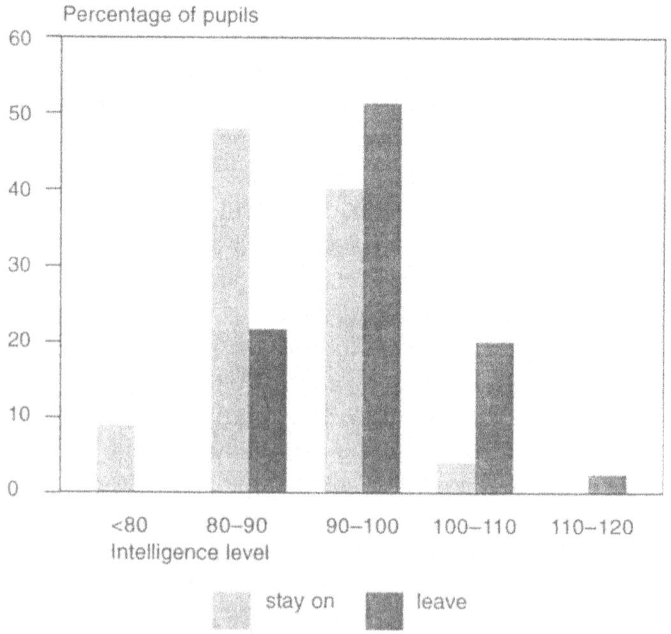

Figure 11.6 Intelligence and the chances of returning

Figure 11.7 Orientation and follow-up of 102 pupils

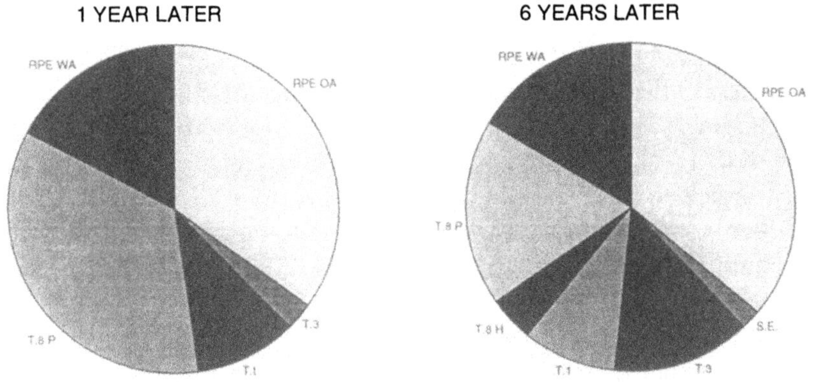

LEGEND:
RPE OA: regular primary education, on advice (PMS & school)
RPE WA: regular primary education, without advice
T.8P: type-8 Parkschool
T.8H: other type-8 (Hasselt)
T.1: B.E. type-1 (light mental retardation)
T.3: S.E. type-3 (emotional/behavioural disorders)
S.E.: secondary education

Figure 11.7 Orientation and follow-up of 102 pupils

Assuming that in type-8 education the teaching objective, i.e. reintegration into mainstream education, can only be attained if the pupil is referred in time, it is of great importance that correct advice is sought at an early stage. Such advice should be clearly outlined. Indeed, insight into the problems involved, information about type-8 education and unanimous advice as to referral, are important factors that can influence the parents in a positive way.

The pupils

'Replacement' affects pupils at two levels. For one thing, their performance at school and their learning attitude are meaningful indicators where reintegration is concerned. For another, the social and emotional aspects can also serve as important criteria for assessment.

At the outset, the newly returned pupils often have a slight head-start over their class mates, as they have just undergone intensive training in the play-learning class. Some pupils feel that by being ahead of the others they have achieved a great success; others might be inclined to over-assess their own abilities.

Both teachers and parents report that slight difficulties in arithmetic, reading and language persist, but that there are no other serious problems on that score. They also point out that problems are more likely to arise where learning attitude and behaviour in class are concerned. Teachers often report that some pupils are easily distracted and show a lack of both attentiveness and motivation; this is a recurrent problem. It should be noted that each time 'returning' a child to mainstream education is recommended, the 'learning attitude' is mentioned as being a risk factor.

Reintegration into a new school generally passes off smoothly; often the pupil returns to the same school where he/she attended pre-school classes.

At first, some pupils have difficulty in adapting to the new class group, but then, other new pupils experience the same difficulties. During that year at school, few social or emotional problems arise, ample proof that a short stay in a special school does not leave a stigma.

The parents

Once the project is under way, parents are placed in a central position. As soon as the pupil is admitted to the play-]earning group, parents are involved in its activities. All parents consider this a great boon.

When the actual 'replacement' has been decided on, the parents have to take on the responsibility. They have to start looking for a new school and making contacts, with some occasional help. According to this operating procedure parents can visit the school as full partners in the cooperation scheme and act accordingly.

The parents are very pleased with this procedure, as they can now act as valid educational representatives of their child when dealing with the teacher. This is why the teacher-parent relationship is so much appreciated by both parties. This does not mean however that contacts between teacher and parents are more frequent than is the case for the other children. Of course, the very nature of their relationship makes for easier liaising between parties, so that the danger of misunderstanding is minimal.

The arrangements agreed upon at the beginning of the school year by the parents, the teacher and the PMS-quidance centre play an important part. Cooperation is encouraged and this clearly gives added value to the whole process.

The teacher

Teachers who work in mainstream education are often unfamiliar with special education. They come into indirect contact with it when a pupil returns from the play-learning class.

The teachers involved think that the introductory talks at the beginning of the school year are an excellent medium for exchanging information about the pupil involved. As a result, mainstream teachers grow more interested in special education and are more open-minded towards it. There is, however, a growing need for direct contact and active cooperation. The same teachers demand more concrete information about the way to approach the pupils, as far as their learning attitude is concerned; they want to know how the special educators succeeded in getting results.

Teachers who are having problems in class with newly returned pupils work out various strategies for dealing with the situation in an appropriate manner. Pupils who experience minor difficulties in connection with their scholastic skills get special attention from the form teacher or are catered for by the remedial teacher. Should a pupil show signs of behavioural disturbance, the teacher him/herself will deal with the problem.

Other data show that a successful integration relies on the outlook and attitude of the teacher, who should be sufficiently informed, feel involved, and should try to establish good contacts with the pupil.

Parents and teachers alike have expressed the need for a play-learning class within a mainstream school. At the moment, setting up such a class does not seem feasible for various reasons. For one thing, the number of pupils in the same school who would benefit from it is not large enough to warrant all the facilities inherent in special education; it would put an enormous strain on the teaching time budget. For another, integrated paramedical support is difficult to organize in a mainstream school. Furthermore, the remedial teacher's stereotyped role consists in solving individual problems, which makes it difficult for him/her to devote much time to supportive action in class. Supportive action is one of the cornerstones of the task entrusted to the Parkschool and in most cases its success is guaranteed. Finally, mainstream education offers less opportunities for cooperating with the parents on issues like acceptance of the child's problems and further supportive action.

The school team

As soon as the pupil's return is decided on, negotiations with the mainstream school start, in order to see if it is prepared to make the extra effort required and if any strategies are planned for dealing with all eventualities. The school management rarely gets involved in the 'replacement' procedure. The follow-up is a job usually left to the form teacher and the remedial teacher. In only a few schools does the management work hand-in-hand with a team of teachers when receiving children with learning difficulties.

The PMS-guidance centres

The PMS-guidance centres are very pleased about the present course of action. They get a lot of queries from teachers who want information on the way special education addresses problems relating to learning attitude. In that area they would welcome the support of special needs staff, whose expert advice would help mainstream teachers to solve future problems concerning other children with difficulties before referral to a special school becomes a matter of urgency.

The replacement procedure is a success. There is only one hitch: the last stage, namely the introductory talk in the new school, is sometimes difficult to arrange for the guidance centre of the special school. It may be possible for the mainstream school's PMS-guidance centre to take the initiative here.

Referral to a play-learning class is found to hinge on a number of factors. Child-related factors, like intelligence, attitude towards work, motivation and functional development deficiencies, and important environmental factors like the family's support capacity and its attitude towards learning and the school in general, can all play a part. At present, however, there is a trend towards earlier referral. Even gifted children, who previously were advised to give the first primary year a try, are now referred to the play-learning class.

Counselling should become part of the standard procedure. In the third year of infant school, in February for instance, the parents could be invited for a discussion of their child's problems, which should be seen in connection with the requirements in the first primary year. Afterwards, parents are in a good position to observe their child at home. If the problems still persist at the end of the third year of infant school, the parents are more willing to accept advice, as they now have a better grasp of the child's difficulties.

Children who, on returning from a special school, are reintegrated in the first primary year, still remain at risk. The attitude of the teacher, and that of the whole school team, determines the reception the child will get and the care he/she will receive. Teacher and team must be prepared to assume a special kind of responsibility for the child involved. Teachers should feel that they are performing efficiently and that they can solve a lot of problems by themselves. That is why they need the support of their colleagues and why joint consultations should be held regularly.

Counsellors in the PMS-quidance centres are very conscious of the fact that the image projected by special education contributes to convincing parents that their child ought to be placed in the play-learning class. The 'Open Door' days, organized with just these parents in mind, are thought to be very helpful. In this context, the first contact with the school, especially with the school management, is all-important.

The PMS-counsellors expect us to refrain from returning pupils who present too great a risk. They say they lack both the time and the know-how needed to counsel mainstream teachers on the approach the latter should use when confronted with such children.

It is therefore important to provide systematic counselling for one whole school year after the pupil's return from the special school. Counselling should address itself to the teachers and the members of the school team, rather than to the individual pupil. This is the only way for mainstream schools to go about setting up the right conditions for the reception of a greater number of children at risk.

Conclusions

As long as the conditions necessary for the adequate reception of children with learning difficulties in a mainstream school are not actually nullified, early but temporary referral to a special school seems indicated in order to ultimately permit the integration of problem pupils in a mainstream school.

The initiative to organize early and temporary special needs education was taken within the context of special education, more specifically because the initial objective of the reintegration idea could not be attained, late referral being common practice.

The current strategy has utterly changed the image of the special school. The stigma traditionally attached to special education does not exist any longer. Referral to a special school is not a measure to be avoided, nor is it to be postponed. Nowadays the special school inspires confidence in the partners in education and in the school guidance services, thus encouraging early orientation and creating real opportunities for cooperation.

Really efficient 'replacement' measures are not taken at the level of the learning difficulties, or at that of the special support given to the pupil; they should be addressed to the teachers and school teams, in fact to the educational system as a whole.

It is important that some of the methods used by special educators are adopted by the mainstream schools. The first step in that direction would be to get the two educational systems to work together each time the return of a pupil is planned.

Ultimate success depends to a large extent on the personality of the teacher and the manner in which he/she tackles such problems as may arise. Further investment in able teachers is required. Key factors in this area are:

- a supportive attitude and a personal interest in pupils with difficulties;
- a school organization offering scope for consultation and cooperation among teachers;
- a curriculum that is not exclusively intended for the average pupil; it should also provide more opportunities for individualization of content and educational strategies;
- the provision of support and specific training for teachers, not only with the view of giving them access to the necessary knowledge and techniques but also, and chiefly, to lend support to the individual and joint feeling of competence.

Perspectives

Coming to the conclusion that early and temporary orientation is an option on which further integration can be based, amounts to arguing in favour of the generalization and the development of the actual operating procedure.

As long as mainstream education fails to provide an adequate reception for *all* children, it is indicated that special education should opt for the early and temporary placement of *all* its pupils. To this end, a number of requirements need to be met:

- As soon as a child is placed in a special school, returning to mainstream education should be put forward as a central theme and kept alive as such. For this purpose, the authorities are expected to take stimulating measures, rather than impose sanctions.

- In mainstream education, an atmosphere of competence must be created; teachers should feel convinced that they are perfectly able to overcome any problems by themselves. A general feeling of competence should prevail; the implication is that policy-makers are expected to take measures to this end and provide in-service training.
- Cooperation among mainstream and special schools should be encouraged; that way, special education can show where its greatest strength lies, and it can pass on its know-how to mainstream education.

References

O'Hanlon C (1993) *Special Education: Integration in Europe,* London: David Fulton.

Ruijssenaars, A. and Counet, E. (1991) 'Special education', in *Education in Belgium: The diverging paths,* OECD: Review of national policies for education. Brussels, Ministerie van de Viaamse Gemeenschap, pp.193–208.

Thys, L. and Van De Ven, G. (1985) *Het eerste leerlaar: de eerste struikelsteen,* Leuven-Amersfoort, Acco.

Van Damme, J. (1992) *Over het aantal iongeren met vertraging in ons onderwils,* Leuven, Research Centre for Secondary and Higher Education, Kathoiieke Universiteit Leuven.

For Product Safety Concerns and Information please contact our EU representative GPSR@taylorandfrancis.com
Taylor & Francis Verlag GmbH, Kaufingerstraße 24, 80331 München, Germany

www.ingramcontent.com/pod-product-compliance
Ingram Content Group UK Ltd.
Pitfield, Milton Keynes, MK11 3LW, UK
UKHW022038061126
477531UK00008B/412
* 9 7 8 1 1 3 8 3 0 4 1 0 9 *